The
SOCIETY
Murders

The
SOCIETY
Murders

The true story of the Wales-King murders

HILARY BONNEY

A Sue Hines Book
Allen & Unwin

A Sue Hines Book
Allen & Unwin Pty Ltd
83 Alexander Street
Crows Nest NSW 2065
Australia
Phone: (61 2) 8425 0100
Fax: (61 2) 9906 2218
Email: frontdesk@allen-unwin.com.au
Web: http://www.allenandunwin.com

National Library of Australia
Cataloguing-in-publication entry:
Bonney, Hilary.
    The society murders.
    Bibliography.
    ISBN 1 74114 120 6.
    1. Wales, Matthew – Trials, litigation, etc. 2. Wales-King,
    Margaret. 3. King, Paul. 4. Trials (Murder) – Victoria.
    5. Parricide. I. Title.
    345.94502523

Cover design by Phil Campbell
Text design & typesetting by Paulina von Goes
Edited by Jo Jarrah
Printed in Australia by Griffin Press

10 9 8 7 6 5 4 3 2 1

Contents

Part Four: Finding

Part Five: Grieving

Part Six: Prosecuting

Part One
Killing

Art thou not content with the stain of
the mother's blood which is on thee?

Menelaus to Orestes in *Euripides,* Orestes

CHAPTER 1

Matthew

4 April 2002

THE DAY HE KILLED HIS MOTHER AND STEPFATHER, MATTHEW Robert Wales spent the afternoon in the white, modern kitchen of his home in Burke Road, Glen Iris cooking them dinner. He washed and chopped vegetables, sautéed onions and stirred stock. He also ground up a large handful of his mother-in-law's blood pressure tablets, stolen the week before, with the Panadeine Forte tablets his wife, Maritza, kept in the medicine cupboard. He crushed the tablets with a spoon on a thick wooden chopping board until they formed a chalky powder. Matthew scraped the powder off the board into a wineglass. Hiding the glass behind some sticky cough mixture bottles in the cupboard above the stove, he returned to his vegetable risotto.

When Domenik woke up, Matthew brought him downstairs for a play in the empty bedroom at the front of the house. An only child, Domenik had enough toys to fill the room. As Matthew watched his son pull toys out of bright plastic tubs, his thoughts were miles away. Seeing Domenik play made him think of his own childhood. That always made him think of his mother, Margaret, and of his stepfather, Paul.

He ran through the list that was always in his head and had been there since he was a little boy. The list of all the things his mother had done to hurt him was long but Matthew knew it well. He thought of all the slights, the manipulations, the giving or withholding of money, the interfering, the conditions she had placed on him, the criticisms, the silences, the pointed remarks, the ostracising, the mind games she had played. He thought of the way his mother had kept him away from his brother and sisters when he was little and how she had not let him visit his real father. He hated the way she treated him – as if he were an idiot or a dumb child instead of a grown man with his own family and his own business. He despised the lack of respect his mother had for Maritza and the superficial way she acted towards Domenik. Margaret had shown nothing but utter contempt for the way he lived his life and the choices he had made.

Earlier in the year, Matthew had been furious with her because she wouldn't let him look at the paperwork for the sale of the Surfers Paradise flat. His grandfather had left the flat for him and the other grandchildren and there had been a real fight about it at the lawyer's office. For a month afterwards, Margaret had not spoken to him. He was so sick of the superior aura she always had. She dominated everything with her moods, her power games and the way she used her money to get leverage. It wasn't just him either – she did it to his sisters and always had done. They were all at her beck and call, not wanting to upset her.

Matthew had a lifetime of lists running through his head. There was almost no room for anything else. When he thought of his mother, Matthew could hardly make sense of the rest of his life.

After he had finished cooking, Matthew went outside and made one more preparation for his mother and stepfather's visit. He took a piece of pine with a rounded end from the pile he had kept in the garage since he moved from Horace Street three months earlier. He hid it in the broom cupboard in the kitchen. That didn't feel right – there was no way he could do anything in front of Maritza. Matthew took the wood outside and hid it behind the small box hedges that grew in a row on both sides of his front door.

Maritza came home from the shop at 5.30 pm and played with Dom. Matthew returned to the kitchen to check on the soup. It was cooked so he poured the chunky vegetable broth into the vitamiser.

Matthew prided himself on his cooking skills. In the sixteen months he had been a househusband there had been little else to congratulate himself about. His sore hand meant that he would never go back to hairdressing and once he had set Maritza up in Maritza's Imports there wasn't too much for him to do other than look after Domenik. Being at home all day was doing his head in – there was too much time to think. That's why he had suggested to Maritza that they sell the shop and give a cafe a go. It would be a bit more social and they could work together. High Street, Armadale couldn't have too many cafes. Six weeks ago, they had put the shop on the market. So far Matthew had talked to a few interested people but nothing concrete had happened yet.

At 6.45 pm Matthew heard his mother's Mercedes slide into the driveway. He had left the gate open for them. Arranging his face into a smile, Matthew went out to greet them. As usual, Margaret was driving. A victim of a few strokes in the past two years, Paul was too doddery to get behind the wheel. He'd had another stroke only two months ago and lately he was looking every one of his seventy-four years.

Once inside, Matthew excused himself and went back into the kitchen. Maritza got the guests a drink. She poured a Chilean red for Paul and a local white for Margaret. While Maritza and

Margaret made small talk in the lounge room, Paul went with Domenik into the toy room.

Matthew thought the soup was ready to serve. He asked his mother and wife to sit at the table and went to get Paul and Domenik. Coming into the toy room, Matthew saw something that made the blood pound in his brain. Paul had his hand down the little boy's nappy. Matthew saw a movie in his mind of himself at seven. A brown-haired boy with a wide smile. Paul King, step-father, husband, manager and gentleman farmer, had his hand down the front of the boy's pants.

Matthew grabbed Domenik and lifted him up into his arms. Ignoring Paul, he took the little boy into the dining room and put him on Maritza's knee before returning to the kitchen, where he poured three bowls of soup. His wife was graced with a small appetite and never ate two courses. Matthew tipped the white powder from the wineglass evenly into two of the bowls. Despite what he thought of them, he didn't want Margaret and Paul to go through any pain – he just wanted to slow them down. He carried their bowls out first. 'You start, I don't want it getting cold.'

Back in the kitchen, Matthew swigged a glass of wine, his mind racing. The list was pulsing in his head again and this time it had Paul in it too and all that stuff from when he was little.

Over dinner they talked about the usual things. Margaret sat at the head of the table. Like a queen, Matthew thought. She did most of the talking. She told him to use his American Express card for the business expenses so that they could get reward points for free holidays. She talked about his four siblings, Sally, Damian, Emma and Prudence, and their children, the garden and the new day care centre Paul was going to every Monday. Margaret said that she wanted to take Domenik on a visit with her to see his cousin who lived nearby. Matthew didn't want his mother or Paul to have anything to do with his son. He could see already that the way his mother treated her grandson was the same way she had treated him when he was little. He despised that.

His mother talked on and on about trivial, everyday things. They never had conversations about the things that really bothered Matthew. Margaret said she needed a holiday because she had a lot going on in her life with all her investments and her social engagements. Matthew didn't have any real idea what she did with her days or her money. His mother never told her children much about her affairs, preferring to keep the financial side of her life very private.

Matthew didn't know what was worse, when his mother didn't speak to him or when she did. Not that he was really listening, his thoughts were going round and round in circles. For different reasons, incapacity and a natural reticence in Paul's case and shyness in Maritza's, the other two at the table were both very quiet. Domenik filled the gaps with his singsong toddler talk.

After eating, the dinner party moved into the lounge room. Maritza went to make cups of chamomile tea with honey while Domenik amused his grandparents. Margaret and Paul kept drinking. Matthew drank with them until the two bottles were finished. His mother was still talking and slurring her words ever so slightly. Paul just sat quietly in a chair next to her. As usual he was in his own world.

At 9.30 pm Domenik started getting ratty, crying and whingeing. Maritza made him a bottle of warm milk and took him by the hand. She and the little boy kissed Margaret and Paul goodnight and went up the stairs to his bedroom.

Margaret put a manicured hand over her mouth, stifling a yawn. She looked at Paul sinking into the armchair. 'We'd better go too.' She helped Paul out of the chair and gathered up her bag and keys. Matthew followed them through the front door.

Once outside, Margaret looked around the front garden of her son's rented house and told him he should tidy it up. Paul walked towards the car. Margaret was a step behind him.

Matthew turned the front light off and felt for the wood hidden behind the box hedges on his right. He lifted the length of pine out of the dirt. With both hands he brought it down on the back of his mother's neck, hard across her silvery blonde hair. She crumpled to the ground without a sound.

Matthew took a step behind Paul, who hadn't heard a thing. Matthew hit him hard with the wood in the same place, across the back of the neck. The old man fell silently face first onto the concrete paving stones.

Matthew hit them again and again on the back of the neck. Each time he brought the wood down a bit harder. He was panting. His mind was a rush of red and he could barely see in front of him. Again and again, harder and harder – until it was all out of him. All those years, he thought, this is for all those years. When blood starting seeping from under the bodies onto the paving, he dropped the piece of wood.

He knelt beside his mother and put his face near her mouth. She had no breath. He touched her wrist, feeling for movement in her veins. There was only stillness. There was blood all over his mother's face and glasses. He knew she was dead.

Matthew leant over his stepfather. He was face down in a puddle of blood and motionless. He felt the old man's wrist – there were no signs of life.

Matthew paced the front yard. Round and round like a mad dog, his chest heaving. He couldn't believe he had done it. All those years of thinking about it and now he had done it. Breathing heavily from emotion and exertion, he ran his hands over his eyes. The bodies were still there, not moving, not making a sound.

He was free. He couldn't think beyond that. The relief washed over him like a wave. Since he was a little kid, he had thought of this and now it was done. All those bloody years, the way she had treated him. Never touching him, never being close to him, all that superficial attention she had given him when really she just wanted to run his life. She had never let him be himself, never let him grow up, and now all that was gone. He was never going to be suffocated by her again.

Matthew looked again at his stepfather, face down on the concrete. Jesus, when he thought of all that stuff the man had done to him. He'd never get to Domenik now.

A flicker of light in the window above the wine shop opposite his house made Matthew look up. A woman was standing there, looking straight at him and talking on the phone. She must have seen him. She was probably calling the cops. He was going to get caught. It didn't seem to matter.

Matthew held his head in his hands. He felt a relief so powerful it was as if every cell in his body had changed its composition. He sat on the front step and looked up at the sky. At that moment all his pain was gone.

He stood up and went inside to find Maritza.

CHAPTER 2

Maritza

4 April 2002

MARITZA WAS UPSTAIRS IN DOMENIK'S BEDROOM WHEN Matthew saw his parents out. Although she found Margaret rather snobby and Paul quiet, the evening had gone smoothly enough. The conversation had been in bits and pieces as it often is with little children around. Domenik had been in a bouncy mood, dancing for his grandmother when she sang 'Twinkle, Twinkle, Little Star'. Paul had played with him too. He'd taken him into the toy room while she talked to Margaret. Domenik liked to show his grandfather different toys and tell him their names. Two-year-olds were always good diversions at family functions. Not that there had been very many family functions with the Wales and the Pizzaros. The two families were separated by a chasm of class and culture that no amount of good manners could close.

At 9.30 pm Domenik, overexcited after being the centre of attention, started crying. Maritza made him say goodnight to Margaret and Paul. He kissed his Nonna, his Pappi and his father and went upstairs. Domenik always went to bed with three toy dogs and a warm bottle of milk. Maritza liked to give him his bottle in her bed to calm him down. Tonight it took a little longer than usual. Still basking in his grandparents' attention, Domenik wanted to keep playing. Maritza turned the lights down low and cuddled the boy while he drank his milk. When he finished, she gathered up her son and lifted him into his own bed. Standing at Domenik's door, she went through their nightly ritual.

'I love you.'

'Bye bye.'

'Bye bye.'

Finally, Domenik called out his last 'bye bye' and went to sleep. Maritza closed his door and went downstairs. The house was dark. The front door was open. The outside light was off. Except for the low hum of traffic in Burke Road, it was quiet. Maritza looked in the lounge room – it was empty. She went out the front door.

The dinner guests were lying in a bloodied heap on the paving. Maritza took a step towards their bodies and then froze. She could walk no closer. She could see what was in front of her but her brain couldn't process the sight. It didn't look real. It looked like something on television. It was not possible that it was real.

Matthew stepped out of the darkness and pushed her inside the house. He was panting. 'Get inside.'

'What happened?'

'I hit them, I hit them. The girl across the road is calling the police.'

Over Matthew's shoulder, Maritza saw that the bodies were still. Matthew pushed her further inside the house and shut the front door. He was shaking and sweaty, his face pale in the dark. There was a red crescent of blood on his tracksuit top.

Maritza ran upstairs and vomited in the toilet. The woman she had been a few seconds earlier, putting her child to bed, had gone.

Her life – as a daughter, a wife and a mother – would never be the same again.

Matthew came into the bathroom and tried to hold her, tried to wipe her face and pull back her long, dark hair. He had blood on his hands. She pushed him away, screaming at him. 'What – what have you done?'

She ran, sobbing, into their bedroom and peered through the curtain. Down in the courtyard, the bodies were still there. Across the road, there was a light in the window of the flat above the wine shop.

'What have you done?'

'I hit them. I hit them. I had to do it. It's like, like . . . a relief. I had it in me. I had to. I had to do it.'

Matthew started talking at her. She couldn't look at him. She couldn't understand what he was saying; she couldn't think past the image of the bodies to understand him. She didn't want to understand him; she didn't want to know what had happened, she wanted to think of nothing. She was scared. Nothing in her life had prepared her for this.

Matthew came towards her with his arms outstretched. 'Do you hate me for this?'

'Don't touch me.' Maritza backed away from him 'I don't want to know. I don't know how I feel. What are you going to do?'

'Just stay here. Just stay here – don't do anything. I'll fix it.'

Matthew went downstairs. Maritza heard him rummaging in drawers and then the front door closing. She pulled the curtains back again and looked down into the front yard. In the glow of the streetlight and the red neon from the Chinese shop across the road, she could see Matthew, wearing a pair of her latex kitchen gloves. He was dragging his mother by her feet to the grass underneath their high, brick front fence. When he got Margaret beside the fence, he turned her over so that she lay face up. Hooking his hands under his stepfather's armpits, Matthew dragged Paul to the same spot.

As she watched, Matthew carried Domenik's blue wading pool, collapsed with exhaustion after the summer, out of the garage. He threw it over the bodies. Maritza could see the bright cartoon faces of the sea creatures printed on the pool – they were smiling. Maritza felt a surge in her stomach. She dropped the curtain and vomited. After that, she didn't look out the window again.

Matthew came back upstairs and told her that he was going to do something about the car. She didn't look at him. She couldn't speak. He ran back downstairs again. She could hear him in the kitchen. The Mercedes' engine started and the automatic gate swung open and then shut with a metallic clang.

Maritza climbed into their bed and pulled the covers over her head. She started crying. All her life she had been a good person, always working, doing the right thing. Nothing had prepared her for this moment. It was a nightmare. It couldn't be real.

A few hours later when Matthew returned, she was in the same position and still awake. Matthew tried to hold her. 'Do you love me?' She turned away from him. He started crying. 'Do you hate me for what I have done?'

Relenting, Maritza embraced her husband's shaking body. 'What are you going to do? What are we going to do?' She cried with him.

When dawn broke on Friday 5 April, Maritza Elizabeth Wales was already locked into a story that was not of her making, but which would lead to her undoing.

Part Two
Living

It sounds like a love story.

Maritza Wales in her Record of Interview
with police on 11 May 2002

CHAPTER 3

Margaret

1933–2002

MARGARET WALES-KING WAS BORN MARGARET MARY LORD IN Yarraville, a cramped and gritty working class suburb on the western side of Melbourne, on 16 June 1933. Six years later her parents, Doreen May Torey and Robert John Lord had another daughter, Diana Agnes. The Lords made a striking family. Rob Lord was a huge man with a personality to match. His wife, known as Dotty, was a tiny woman with great spirit. Their daughters were fair-headed and pretty.

Rob Lord was a truck driver who made a fortune through road construction in the suburbs of Melbourne. During the thirties and forties, Lord's business expanded rapidly. By the 1960s his company, Victoria Roads Ltd, was one of Victoria's largest road contractors and the first to use hot mix asphalting in road construction. The growth of the Melbourne suburbs in the post-war years meant that Lord became rich. When he retired, he owned quarries in Braybrook and Greensborough in Victoria and in Western Australia.

When the Lord girls were young, their father moved the family across the city, and up a few social rungs, to the leafy affluence of

Camberwell. Margaret and Diana grew up in the genteel eastern suburb wanting for nothing. Margaret attended boarding school in junior school and then completed her secondary schooling at Loreto Mandeville Hall, a private girls' school in Toorak. When she left the sheltered world of Mandeville, Margaret attended business school but never followed a commercial career. She had a strong interest in the arts which she maintained her whole life. Her passions were painting, drawing and interior decorating.

Tall and attractive, Margaret Lord was a success in the Melbourne social scene during the 1950s. Soon after the break-up of another relationship, she met a dashing pilot called Brian Wales. 'Biggles' Wales was the eldest son of John Wales of Strathmore, a suburb on the other side of town from Camberwell. The pair married the day after Margaret's twenty-fourth birthday, 17 June 1957, at Our Lady of Victories Catholic Church in Burke Road, Camberwell. Margaret wore a white French corded satin gown and carried gold roses. Her face was covered with a fingertip tulle veil held with a pearl coronet perched in her upswept blonde hair. The bridesmaids, her sister and Barbie Hume, wore ballerina frocks of blue French faille embossed with white. The wedding party visited Margaret's old school, Mandeville Hall, before enjoying a reception at a ritzy reception centre known by its address – 9 Darling Street, South Yarra.

When they returned from their honeymoon, Margaret and her new husband moved into her parents' home at 4 Marlborough Avenue, Camberwell. Her bridesmaid, Barbie Hume, and the comedian Barry Humphries lived in the same street. Rob and Dotty Lord conveniently moved out to the neighbouring suburb of Balwyn. Soon the family home filled with five children – Sally Anne (born 10 September 1958), Damian John (born 11 March 1960), Emma Jane (born 13 July 1963), Prudence Kate (born

24 May 1965) and Matthew Robert (born 18 February 1968). The Wales family lived comfortably, dividing their time between their Camberwell home, a holiday house in Skelton Lane at Sorrento, an uppercrust seaside village on the Mornington Peninsula, and a flat in Twin Towers apartments at Mount Buller in the Victorian ski fields.

Margaret's younger sister, Di, married Tony Yeldham, a Sydney man who owned a high fashion business called The Squire Shop. The Yeldhams quickly became fixtures in the Sydney social scene. Years later the name would become known for less glamorous reasons as Tony's brother, David, a Supreme Court judge, gained notoriety by killing himself in 1996 when allegations of paedophilia were made against him.

Di and Tony had three children, Ali, Rebecca and Joshua, and then divorced. At the time of her sister's murder, Di Yeldham was a regular in the Sydney social pages and the owner of Art House Gallery in Rushcutters Bay with her daughter Ali. Rebecca was working in the film industry and Joshua was, at thirty-one, a darling of the Australian modern art world, winning awards and accolades for his paintings and short films.

In 1968, the Wales family took a holiday on Brampton Island in Queensland that was to change their lives. Paul King, a dapper and single businessman, was also holidaying on the island. He was travelling alone and struck up a friendship with Brian Wales. The two men were of a similar age and lived near each other in Melbourne. The friendship expanded to include Margaret and endured for many years despite Brian, who was a pilot with TAA, one of the two domestic airlines operating at the time, frequently travelling for long periods of time. Damian Wales recalls that when his father was away, Paul King, the 'family friend', spent an 'inappropriate' amount of time with his mother.

When he was home, Brian had more than a few arguments with Margaret in the years that followed their Brampton Island holiday. Eventually, Margaret Wales started a sexual relationship with Paul King.

Emma Connell remembers that Paul would come to the beach house at Sorrento or to the snow with her family. She first twigged that something was going on between her mother and the quiet family friend when she was about eight. One night in 1971, Emma followed her mother out of the house. Although her father was away, Emma's mother was all dressed up with somewhere to go. Keeping out of sight, Emma watched as Margaret stepped into a car driven by Paul King and was whisked away. The little girl ran back to the house and told Marion, the nanny, that her mother had gone. Marion was angry with her young charge and sent her off to bed. As Emma puts it, 'From then on we didn't see Paul for a long time.' Looking back, Emma realised that her mother was 'sneaking off to see Paul and Marion was giving Pa Lord the rundown ... Pa ultimately spoke to Mum who I know was told in no uncertain terms to keep away from Paul or she would lose her inheritance. The next time I saw Paul was in the back row of Pa's funeral and I would have been about twelve. The subject was never mentioned again and Marion actually left either that night or a few nights later and I've never seen her again.'

Rob Lord died in 1974 and, with the bulk of her inheritance secure, Margaret was finally able to let her relationship with Paul King become public. Within days of Lord's funeral, Brian Wales moved out of the family home to the Sorrento beach house and Paul King moved in with Margaret and the five children. Eventually, a devastated Brian petitioned for a divorce because he thought that Margaret acted like she didn't want one. In 1976, the

Wales's divorce became final – Sally was seventeen, Damian fifteen, Emma twelve, Prudence was ten and Matthew just seven. Despite her late husband's views of the affair, Dotty Lord continued to visit her daughter and the family until her death in 1978.

The older Wales children bore the brunt of their father's depression and were unwillingly cast as his counsellors, enduring long conversations with him about the loss of his adored wife. Margaret agreed that Brian could have unlimited access to the children. The four eldest often stayed at Sorrento with him for weekends and school holidays. Matthew, a beautiful boy with a cheeky grin, was treated differently from his siblings. He was held back by his mother and not offered the unlimited access the others enjoyed with their father. Emma describes Matthew as 'a bit of a pawn in the divorce game ... Mum being conscious of the fact that Paul didn't have any children, tried very hard to fill that void with Matthew, and Paul was very much his father figure.'

Brian Wales remembers that 'I did not have much to do with Matthew. I felt that this was mainly because Margaret and Paul wanted it to look like Matthew was their child. I know that at some stage after our separation Matthew, who was only fairly young, was receiving treatment from a psychologist for behavioural problems.'

Brian remembers the period after the separation as one with a few difficulties. He was able to visit the children in Camberwell but Margaret would stay in the house while he did so. On one occasion, Margaret told Brian that Paul would be a better father to Matthew than he would and that she did not want Brian to exercise any fatherly influence over their youngest son.

Despite this, Brian remained on good terms with Margaret until he married an Englishwoman called Geraldine in 1985. He has lived in the United Kingdom since 1993. When Margaret and

Paul went missing, Brian Wales, then seventy-five, took the long flight from Heathrow to be with his children. When his ex-wife's body was found, he went to her rosary, funeral and memorial services. He also visited his son in jail.

Margaret and Paul enjoyed a comfortable life and were considered by their friends to be great lovers. Soon after they started living together, the family moved into Talbot Crescent in Kooyong, a suburb not far, geographically or demographically, from Camberwell. When he joined the Wales family, Paul King had a farm near Kyneton, a quaint country town an hour and a half north of Melbourne, on which he ran Angus cattle. The children and Margaret used to travel there with him for weekends. Paul worked at Coats Paton as an advertising manager and Margaret lived on the large inheritance she received from her father.

The disbursement of Pa Lord's estate meant that the younger three children had a more privileged upbringing than their older brother and sister. They had everything they wanted. Prudence kept three horses at the family's farm at Balnarring, across the Mornington Peninsula from Sorrento, and remembers Matthew having several motorbikes. She felt that 'During this period of our lives Mother was really generous and we were very spoiled.' Emma also remembers the family's lifestyle at this time as very privileged. 'Mum was very generous and we never wanted for anything. We had a beach house, we had a unit at the snow, we had several farms with animals, horses and had some pretty amazing trips overseas ...'

Emma recalls her mother not being very strict: 'she was very loving and caring and ... carefree.' Margaret 'was always very spontaneous and we'd just up and do something. She'd always be very supportive of anything you wanted to do. She had an arty, laid-back, almost hippie, like really cool, calm and collected disposition. She loved to paint and she'd paint with all her hippie arty friends but she also used to take us all along and we'd all have an easel and paint with her.' In among the free times, there were certain rules. Margaret was also known at home as 'the one who must be obeyed'.

The children went to expensive private schools scattered throughout the eastern suburbs. The girls went to their mother's old school, Loreto Mandeville Hall. Damian was sent to Xavier College and Matthew to the Malvern campus of Caulfield Grammar School.

Margaret's carefree existence was challenged by the onset of breast cancer when she was in her forties. She had surgery on both breasts and an implant in one. She survived the horrors of cancer treatment to live in full remission for nearly another three decades.

For a decade from 1990, Margaret and Paul added the care of Margaret's elderly aunt, Elsie Lucia McCandlish, known as 'Lully', to their family responsibilities. Lully, the undisputed matriarch of the Lord families, was a source of wisdom and support for Margaret and Di until she died aged 101 in 2000.

By 1995, all of the Wales children had moved out of home. Margaret and Paul celebrated by eloping to Queensland. Di Yeldham found out her sister had remarried when she and Paul came to Sydney on the way home and she saw new wedding rings on their fingers.

The couple bought a more streamlined, modern home at 40 Mercer Road, Armadale and kept a property in Thomas Street in Red Hill South, a rural wine-growing area filled with country retreats for tired Melburnians, halfway down the Mornington Peninsula. They commuted between the two properties and kept busy socialising. Margaret had a large network of friends and an extensive share portfolio to tend. Their two homes and gardens were maintained in immaculate condition. Margaret continued to paint and draw in oils and watercolours and, inspired by her gardens, grew especially fond of botanical subjects. Mercer Road received the benefit of Margaret's constant interest in decorating and art and antique collecting. At the time of her death, the contents of Margaret's home, including her antiques, were worth approximately $800 000.

In 2000, Margaret and Paul's relationship underwent a seismic shift when Paul became seriously ill. He collapsed at the Red Hill property and was rushed to the closest hospital by ambulance. The doctors diagnosed a heart condition and a subsequent cerebral bleed. Paul was released to a rehabilitation hospital for intensive therapy. Over the following two years, Paul was rendered more and more incapacitated by further cerebral bleeds. At seventy-four, Paul King was physically frail and mentally diminished. Alzheimer's disease was making him easily confused and forgetful. As his stepdaughter Sally said, he 'just wasn't the man he was'.

As Paul became progressively worse, Margaret found herself responsible for his constant care. Paul was becoming a risk to himself and others, doing things like leaving the gas on and forgetting about it. Margaret, who was conscious of safety at the best of times, was unable to leave her husband unsupervised. After nearly thirty years of being an adored and pampered wife, Margaret was forced to become a nurse and nanny. She did not enjoy the change of role. Margaret's life had become limited by the changes in Paul and she was finding it difficult to care for him. She felt that she had lost her companion because Paul could not talk with her about anything of substance. She was besieged with worry about him. She stopped travelling too far from the Cabrini Hospital in Malvern for fear that Paul would collapse again and be unable to receive the appropriate medical attention quickly. When she placed him in a nursing home for a few days' respite, she returned to find him wandering the streets in his dressing gown, completely disorientated. At the time of her murder, Margaret was making inquiries about moving Paul permanently into a nursing home on the corner of Burke and Toorak Roads in Camberwell. For an attractive woman used to an easy life, being more of a nurse than a wife was just too difficult.

All of the Wales children married. Margaret's daughters were in their second marriages and, between them, had seven young children. Matthew and his three sisters lived within a five-kilometre radius of their mother's home. The daughters visited their mother quite often and rang her frequently. Margaret saw Matthew and his family about once a month for a meal.

Damian Wales moved to Sydney when he was twenty-six and, after his marriage to Elizabeth, decided to stay there. The couple has three young boys. Damian works as a financial trader and Liz looks after the boys.

Margaret helped her children to buy their family homes by setting up trusts in each child's name and lending them money. The distribution of Margaret's wealth was a sensitive subject in the Wales family. Some of the family, including Matthew, for whom the feeling became a murderous obsession, felt that their mother used her money to control them. Sally felt that, to a certain extent, her mother used her will to dominate her and some others in the family.

Prue agreed. 'As we got older and wanted to be more independent, Mum started withholding financial support as a means of controlling us and getting us to do what she wanted us to.' Prue also found that it was not unusual for her mother to control situations with money. She said that things were either done her mother's way or not at all and that her mother could be very unreasonable at times.

Emma didn't share her sisters' feelings. She thought that her mother was overprotective about the family wealth but attributed that to her mother being too astute to let her children jeopardise it. From the break-up of her first marriage, Emma learnt how her mother could step in to protect her investments when difficult situations arose. Margaret was almost paranoid about outsiders taking advantage of her family's wealth and took steps to protect it when they each separated from their first husbands.

Emma's second husband, James Connell, had a different, outsider's view of his mother-in-law's relationship with her children. In a statement to police made just after she went missing, he said that 'She has demonstrated time and time again that she can play the hard ball when it lands in her court. Which has frustrated ... all of her children at one time or another. To the best of my knowledge all of the children and their respective spouses have effectively insulated themselves from being emotionally blackmailed by Margaret. Matthew, due to his financial situation, is still at her beck and call. From my point of view, I feel she can be really unfair and seems to love the self-importance of being in control. I would further say that all the children, excepting Matthew, have now obtained financial independence and as such are no longer under her control in regards to financial matters.'

Angus Reed, another of Margaret's sons-in-law, shared James's view of her. 'I would say that Margaret tried to manipulate her children through the use of money. I used to tolerate her and would say that I was indifferent towards her.' Reed was positive about Margaret's abilities as a grandmother.

Matthew's siblings felt that he had received more help than any of them and thought that he did so because he was the weakest child in the litter. While Sally thought that Matthew always had his hand out, he told the police that Sally had received the most help of any of the children. Sally's views of Matthew and Margaret's relationship were echoed by her other siblings. Prudence said, 'When he became a teenager, their relationship deteriorated because of Matthew's lack of responsibility. My mother still wanted to control Matthew, and protect him because she thought he wasn't able to stand on his own two feet. Mother was different to Matthew than she was to the rest of us. She gave him more time and money because she believed that he did not have the ability to get on. She seemed to make more allowance for Matthew and cover up for his inadequacies.'

Damian thought that Matthew acted like a 'puppy' to their mother. He said that his younger brother completely relied on her and that Margaret had 'forked out money for him for ages'. Matthew was 'so lovey, lovey to her, almost to the point of being a suck. I was always of the opinion that he never really left her breast – always clinging on to her'. He felt that Margaret had had enough of Matthew's dependency on her and that she wanted to cut him off so that he gained some independence. For this reason, Damian thought that his mother was keen to see her youngest child married. 'I think basically she was fed up with supporting him both emotionally and financially.'

Margaret was conscious of preserving the fortune her father had left her for the next generation. She executed her last will on 17 August 1990. In it she made her two sons and family solicitor, Tony Joyce, executors. She provided that Paul King's unmarried sister, Mary King, would have her living expenses paid until her death and that the rest of her estate would be divided into six equal shares between her partner and children. Her children's shares contained an unusual condition. Each child had to make it to forty before collecting their inheritance. Even from the grave, Margaret wanted to ensure that her money was used with some degree of maturity.

Fifteen days before she was killed, Margaret Wales-King asked her faithful family solicitor to draft a new will. Tony Joyce took instructions from Margaret and sent her a draft will for consideration. Sally and Damian Wales found the document in their mother's filing cabinet after she went missing. Before they read it, they were ignorant about what their mother wanted to do with her fortune after she died. The draft will was even more restrictive than her current will. In it, Margaret stipulated that all her children were to be her executors and that Paul would be looked after during his lifetime. On his death, Margaret wanted six trusts created. The first would be a special trust with a bequest of $200 000 for Emma's daughter from her first marriage. That trust would last until she turned thirty. The other five will trusts were for each of Margaret's children. Each child would receive an equal share of the remaining estate. Once again, Margaret had included a condition – the Wales siblings were not to get a cent of their mother's capital until she had been dead for ten years. For some reason, Margaret had felt the need to keep an even tighter rein on her wealth. She was murdered before she could ensure that happened.

CHAPTER 4

Paul

1927–2002

PAUL ALOYSIUS KING WAS BORN IN SYDNEY ON 26 OCTOBER 1927, the second of four children. His brother Stephen was older and brother Peter and sister Mary were younger. It seems that Paul King was a person who lived for nearly three-quarters of a century without leaving much trace on the earth. He had no natural children or grandchildren, few relatives apart from his elderly siblings and their children and no friends independent of those made through his wife. When he fell ill in 2000 with a heart condition, Paul's only hospital visitors were people his wife knew.

Stephen King was seventy-six when his younger brother disappeared. A Roman Catholic priest living in a Marist community in Sydney's northern suburbs, he described his murdered brother as a reticent person who would not have wanted anything written about him. The way Paul King lived his life, with few demands and no fanfare, ensures that Paul's wish for privacy will be respected, more by necessity than good manners. In all the media reports of the Wales-King murders, there is little mention of Paul King's history and background. It is as if he had no presence apart from his role of husband to Margaret. In fact, falling in love with the beautiful, wealthy Margaret was the most dramatic thing he did in his quiet life. The relationship would ultimately grant the loyal and quiet husband a most unquiet death.

Until the early 1960s, Paul worked in the wool industry in Sydney. At that time, he was employed by Coats Paton, a pattern and wool manufacturing company, and was given the opportunity to move to Melbourne to take up the position of Advertising Manager for Australia. Paul took the job and moved into a small, simply furnished flat in Prahran. He stayed at Coats until his early retirement, at fifty, in 1977. When he left the firm he was the State Manager for Victoria. One of his work colleagues described Paul as 'one of God's gentlemen' and said that he conducted his life with incredible dignity. His employees recalled him as a very considerate and respectful manager who was always well spoken and well dressed. His devotion to his wife was legendary. Margaret persuaded Paul to retire early so that he could work with her managing her bookwork and breeding Angus cattle on their farm.

Depending on their birth order, the Wales children had either an outright disregard or a resigned indifference to their mother's husband. The older Wales children had little respect for Paul. In their statements they referred to him as 'the Butler', 'the Shadow'. Off the record, they told police that their nickname for him was 'the Poof'. Damian and Sally perceived Paul to be the cause of their parents' divorce. Sally says that she has 'never really forgiven Paul for what I believe was the reason for my mother and father separating and eventually divorcing'.

Damian recalls that when his father moved out and Paul moved in to the family home in Camberwell in 1976, the older children did not want him there. He told police that he had found out that his stepfather had completed a Dale Carnegie course on 'How to Win Friends and Influence People' and that in his view,

Paul was trying to improve himself by putting on airs and graces and cultivating a debonair image.

After his disappearance, Emma said that:

Paul has always been there – he's always been part of our lives … it was like he was an extension of Mum. I got on very well with Paul – I've never had a problem with him. He tried very hard to help Mum control us kids in the kindest way and I must admit we didn't pay much attention to him. We didn't pay much attention to him because he was a real softie – but Mum was the one who "must be obeyed". Because we had such close contact with our father we didn't want Paul to be a father figure – he was more Mum's partner and a lot of the time considered [to be] Mum's driver. He was there at Mum's beck and call and he was only trying to appease her. He didn't insist on us appeasing him – he was really there to provide Mum with moral support.

Paul had a closer relationship with the younger Wales children. Prue remembers that:

Paul was especially good to Matthew and myself. I believe that because Sally, Damian and Emma were all older, they had a greater bond to my father and did not accept Paul so readily. Over the years, Paul was a real father figure to Matthew and they were very close. He was very patient and fair with Matthew. This relationship changed over time. As Matthew got older he lost respect for Paul. I believe this was because Paul was so controlled by my mother and he never stood up for himself … when we were very young … he paid us both equal attention.

Prue said that although her stepfather didn't have any friends, he was delightful and very polite. 'He was considerate.'

The Wales-King relationship was one in which Paul catered to Margaret's every whim. Prue observed that it 'was very loving. Paul was like a slave and he did everything for her ... Mum would sometimes be the most shocking bitch to him but he would take it'.

When Paul became ill, he required care and Margaret was required to supply it. It was a change of dynamic that did not sit easily with Margaret Wales-King. She complained about having to care for her husband and the curbing of her social life to her daughters. Emma said, 'Mum had often spoken about her concerns for what she was going to do with Paul ... He required Mum's full time care which was an absolute 360 because before his strokes he did everything for Mum, she was treated like a princess by him. Mum found it very hard to cope because she had always been very indulged.'

Paul King did not have the wealth his wife had. When he died he owned a joint shareholding with Margaret of about $88 000 and had a small credit balance in his everyday bank account in the ANZ at Malvern. The house in Armadale was in Margaret's name. His wife left an estate worth over six million dollars.

In Paul's will, made in April 1990, the bequests he makes reveal something of his true feelings about Margaret's family. Paul left $2500 to each of his brothers. He provided that Damian, Emma and Prudence each receive the same amount. Matthew Wales was to inherit $10 000. The rest of Paul's estate was to provide income for Paul's unmarried sister Mary and then, after her death, to be divided equally between Matthew Wales, Emma's daughter from her first marriage and the Little Sisters of the Poor in Randwick, Sydney. Sally Wales was not left anything.

During the investigation of his murder, the Homicide Squad became aware of allegations that Paul King had sexually abused Matthew. Matthew's brother and sisters were asked their views. Each of them denied that it was a possibility.

Prue said that 'To the best of my knowledge Paul never abused Matthew either physically or mentally. Paul was a very gentle and caring person and he never laid a hand on us. I believe that if Paul had ever abused Matthew in any way, I would have been aware of it. If my mother had ever become aware of Paul abusing Matthew in any way I am confident that she would have terminated their relationship straight away.'

Damian Wales had similar views. 'My personal view is that I have never seen any signs of such behaviour in Paul ... had Matthew ever mentioned it to Mum, she would have stood behind her children rather than Paul. She would not be the type of mother who would turn a blind eye and hide from the truth. She would always back her children first – they were number one in her life and had Matthew mentioned it to her, Paul would have been booted out on his ear, as well as reported to police and Matthew would know this. In regard to talk of my mother physically abusing Matthew that is a load of rubbish.'

In his record of interview, Matthew said that, even though he liked Paul, he killed him because he caused the disintegration of his parents' marriage. He told Ian Joblin, his forensic psychologist, that he killed his mother and Paul on 4 April 2002 because that was the evening he saw Paul King with his hand down his two-year-old son's nappy. Matthew also told Joblin that Paul had sexually abused him for years and that he was too humiliated to tell police about the abuse during his record of interview.

Only Matthew knows the truth.

CHAPTER 5

Love

MATTHEW WALES AND MARITZA PIZZARO MET IN 1997 BECAUSE of an act of vanity. If Maritza had not wanted to tame her naturally curly hair, she would not have become a co-defendant in a murder case. Matthew was a hairdresser who was good at making the wavy sleek and Maritza was a shop assistant who found a hairdresser she liked talking to. Their different ages, and social and cultural backgrounds meant that their paths would have been unlikely to cross anywhere outside the Hairhouse Warehouse salon in Knox City Shopping Centre.

Maritza Wales was born on 29 August 1963 in Santiago, Chile to Honoria and Mario Pizzaro. Her thirty-year-old parents already had two children, Mario and Patricia. Mario senior worked as a fitter and turner and Honoria looked after the children. On 26 November 1976, the same year that the Wales's divorce became final, the Pizzaro family migrated to Australia, leaving the horrors of Pinochet's dictatorship in Chile, an extended family and a house behind them.

When the Pizzaros arrived with dreams of a better life in a democracy, they stayed in the far-flung eastern Melbourne suburb of Mitcham, living firstly in a migrants' hostel and then in a rented house. Maritza, who was thirteen, and her sister settled in to study at Aquinas College, a Catholic school in Ringwood. To help their transition to a new culture, the girls went to English classes in the evenings.

At seventeen, Maritza left school to become a student of book-keeping at Hollingworth Business College. For two years she took shorthand, typing and commercial English classes in order to get a job in an office.

In 1982, Maritza found her first job as a receptionist at the Eastern Youth Centre in Heathmont. The centre helped disadvantaged youth and Maritza enjoyed the work. Even though she had started work, Maritza continued living at home with her parents and sister. Her brother, Mario, had recently married and moved out.

In 1983, the Eastern Youth Centre had funding problems and Maritza was retrenched. She found a job as a clerical assistant in the classifieds department of the *Age* newspaper. Little did she know that twenty years later, the same newspaper would feature her picture on its cover many times. For more than nine years Maritza worked steadily in the job. Spurning her imminent entitlement to long service leave, she resigned just before her ten-year anniversary to join her parents in Chile. Mario and Honoria had returned to their homeland because Pinochet had been overthrown and Chile was beginning to flourish under the leadership of its newly elected president, Patricio Aylwin. After a year, despite the positive economic climate in their native country, the Pizzaros returned to settle in Melbourne. Mario and Honoria bought a home in Kanooka Road, Boronia, a lower middle class suburb full of cheap housing, 25 kilometres south east of the city. Their daughters moved with them.

Maritza, who was then thirty-one, got a job working as a sales assistant in the ladies' fashion section of Myer's department store in outer eastern suburban Knox City Shopping Centre. It was while working there that Maritza discovered a hairdresser, Michael, who was both good at his job and convenient. He worked in a salon called Hairhouse Warehouse in the same centre. When Maritza moved from Myer's to the Bally shoe store in the city and then to Alberto Piazza shoes in inner-suburban Carlton, she kept going to the salon in Knox City.

One day in 1997, Michael couldn't keep his weekly appointment with Maritza, so he asked his colleague to do her hair. Maritza liked the way Matthew Wales made her hair smooth but not too straight. She changed hairdressers. After a few months of twice-weekly appointments, the client and the hairdresser became good friends. 'He used to talk about his girlfriend and – and I was – he always used to – he used to do my hair. He used to perve on my top. I never had anything there.' She didn't have a boyfriend, but she did have a girlfriend who was trying to get her one. The friend had arranged a blind date between Maritza and a Spanish man. Maritza decided she needed to get her hair done for the occasion. She rang Matthew and asked him to do her hair the next day. Matthew agreed to work late to fit her in. Maritza invited him back to the family home for dinner after the appointment.

Maritza had the house to herself. Her parents were in Chile on an extended holiday and her sister had moved out. Over dinner, Matthew asked her why she didn't already have a lover and about the blind date the next night. Maritza told him that she wasn't really looking for anyone. After talking for hours, Matthew said he should be getting home. It was 2 am. Maritza didn't want Matthew to ride his motorbike home in the dark. She had had two friends who had been killed in a motorbike accident. She asked him to stay and return in the daylight. Matthew spent that night in Maritza's parents' bedroom. Alone. The next morning he told Maritza that he had the best night's sleep of his life. When he saw her dressed for work wearing high heels, he told her she had great legs.Within two months they were an item. Four months after that, they moved in together. Matthew was twenty-nine. Maritza was thirty-four.

*

Matthew Wales was born in Melbourne on 18 February 1968. With perfect features and an angelic face, he quickly became the apple of his mother's eye. When a severe case of peritonitis threatened Matthew's life at six weeks, his position as 'golden boy' and special baby of the family was secured. The illness also meant that Matthew received extra attention from an early age. Emma was four when Matthew came home from hospital. She remembers him as an adorable, beautiful looking little boy, his mother's aesthetic masterpiece.

The beautiful boy was not without his faults. When Matthew started school, first at Loreto Mandeville Hall's pre-school and then at Caulfield Grammar School's Malvern junior campus, it became clear that whilst the genetic lottery had given him a double helping of looks, he had been dealt a half-serve of brains. Matthew was diagnosed as having learning difficulties and spent some time with teachers and psychologists trying to overcome his deficiencies.

Matthew struggled with school until he left, after finishing Year 11 at Caulfield Grammar School. His school marks were consistently appalling and well below average. One of his teachers in Year 10 remarked in a school report that Matthew was wasting his and everyone else's time both in class and out of it. After going

to Taylor's College for a short and unproductive time, Matthew
finished school in 1985. He was seventeen.

As she had done for most things in his life, Margaret Wales-
King arranged her youngest son's first job. Matthew lasted four
months before being sacked from his position as a storeman at
McEwan's hardware store.

He decided to study hairdressing at the John Morey School of
Hairdressing. John Morey was a 'celebrity' hairdresser. Matthew
completed the twenty-month course and secured his first job with
John Morey at his salon. Matthew's sisters were under the impression that their mother paid for Matthew to complete the course.
He denies that was the case and says that he enjoyed the study and
found hairdressing creative. After a year with John Morey,
Matthew went to work for another up-market hairdresser, Peter
Sango, at his Toorak Road, South Yarra salon. Matthew was not
progressing well in his job and rumour has it that his mother
secretly paid his wages for a few months to encourage Sango to
keep her son on. In any event, after a year Sango's largesse came to
an end. For the next year Matthew worked for 'Karl of
Switzerland'. He then moved to Latouff International at Knox
City Shopping Centre and stayed there for five years. After a short
stint in Queensland, Matthew returned to work for Latouff at
Doncaster Shopping Town in the less leafy eastern suburbs.

In March 1997, Tony Latouff offered Matthew a sub-lease on
the back half of his shop at Knox City Shopping Centre. Matthew
took up the opportunity and ran a successful four chair salon. He
employed a few staff and made himself between $1500 and $3000
a week. He managed to save $20 000 which he gave to his mother
to mind for him in her bank safety deposit box. At last, Matthew
felt proud of himself. Perhaps he wasn't as dumb as his family
thought he was.

Matthew never felt that his brother and sisters respected him. When he was sixteen, at the behest of his mother, he saw a clinical psychologist, Raymond Smith. Margaret and Paul were concerned that Matthew lacked direction, motivation and maturity. Matthew told Smith that he felt marginalised and denigrated by his siblings. Smith found a boy who was immature and not blessed with self-management skills. He also found that the family had one touchy issue – the distribution of Margaret's wealth to the children.

Certainly the Wales's privileged upbringing did not protect them from anger and disaffection. Damian was never close to his younger brother. He thought Matthew 'was a prick of a kid ... reckless and irresponsible' who was always lying and was often cruel to animals. It was Damian's view that Matthew had the support of their mother no matter what his behaviour and that, from his earliest years, he played a 'snide and cunning game'. Sally shared Damian's distrust of their younger brother and had disliked him since she could remember.

When Matthew was a baby, Emma used to spend a lot of time playing with him. As he got older she grew less fond of him. She found his cruel antics with animals at the family farm too hard to stomach. She thought that the teenage Matthew, who had become more secretive and cunning, was worse.

Prue thought that her little brother was strange. He crucified flies when he was four and impaled eels when he was eight. At ten, he tied mice by their tails to the back of his motorbike and drove around the farm in Balnarring until the body of the mouse dislocated from the tail.

When they were growing up, the Wales children were always having fights with Matthew. In Emma's words, 'We all seemed to be disappointed in him most of the time.'

When he met Maritza, Matthew lived in a single-fronted weatherboard cottage at 6 Horace Street, Malvern. The property had been bought for him by the Matthew Wales Trust, a family trust established by his mother for his benefit when he was eighteen. The trust bought the house for $236000. Margaret financed $150000 of the purchase price and a loan was taken out with the ANZ bank for the rest. She had done the same for each of her children.

Before he met Maritza, Matthew liked to party hard and chase the girls. After a three year relationship, he was engaged briefly to Fleur Lauber, an attractive blonde with a similar pedigree to his own. A week after deciding to marry Lauber, Matthew changed his mind. His mother, much to his annoyance, kept in contact with Lauber long after her relationship with Matthew lost its ardour. Matthew believed that Margaret felt Lauber was the daughter-in-law she should have had.

Matthew had different ideas about his choice of life partner. He quickly became absolutely besotted with Maritza. He was in no hurry for her to meet his family. He told her they were not like a real family but were snobs who competed with each other about their money. On the way to finally introduce his mother and step-father to Maritza's parents, Margaret complained to her son that she was worried about driving to Boronia and leaving her Mercedes parked there. Matthew told Maritza that his family thought hers were 'just a bunch of wogs'.

Matthew's three sisters did not exactly clasp their brother's girlfriend to the bosom of their family. Margaret, Paul and Emma first met Maritza at the same time. Emma was surprised to find her 'very shy and quiet' because her brother had not described her that way. She said that when her parents left 'the façade lifted and she seemed like a common vulgar little guttersnipe, really –

I couldn't believe how much of a chameleon she was. She would say some shocking things and everything seemed to have a sexual connotation. She thought she was a sex kitten.' Sally also thought that Maritza made unwarranted sexually suggestive comments.

Despite the lack of an immediate connection between the two families, Matthew married his older, olive-skinned, Chilean girl-friend on 16 May 1998 at Flinders Catholic Church on the Mornington Peninsula. The wedding cost the couple $25 000 they didn't have. They were still paying off the loan, in monthly instal-ments, three years later.

Emma didn't think her brother and Maritza had a very equal marriage. 'She totally dominated him from the moment they met.' Sally and Prue's observations were that Matthew was totally dominated by his wife. Sally told police that 'He has got a sub-servient nature and actually calls Maritza "Mamma", as if she's his mother. He does everything she tells him to ... what to eat, the way he dresses, what he wears, the way he looks after Domenik. I believe he's frightened of her, he wishes to please her at every turn – I think he's besotted by her.'

Prue says that Maritza often told her that she had 'Matthew by the balls' and that he would do everything she asked. Whenever Prue was with Matthew alone, he would call Maritza and tell her where he was and who was with him.

Emma recalled an incident when she was visiting her brother and Maritza hit Matthew across the head because he was smoking. Emma said Maritza said to her, 'I have that man by the balls – I won't have my man smoking. You have to have your guy by the balls. He needs a damn good belting now and then ... Matty really gets it from me. I'm tough and he deserves it.'

Damian Wales hadn't forged a strong bond with his sister-in-law either. His lack of affection for his brother prevented them spending much time together. He told police that, in the first days after the disappearance, he visited Matthew and Maritza's house looking for a recent video of Margaret and Paul to give to the media. Damian was disturbed by Maritza's behaviour. She couldn't look him in the eye nor did she seem upset by her in-laws vanishing. Damian had to use the bathroom while he was at Burke Road. As he hadn't been there before, Maritza said she'd show him where it was. He told police that 'When we got to the bathroom, I walked in and as she went to close the door she said to me, "Do you want me to hold it?" obviously referring to my penis. I was flabbergasted by that comment – it was so strange in the circumstances and seems even more so now, given what we know.'

Prue told police that Maritza was nice to Margaret and Paul but behind their backs was very insulting about them. Emma said that not long after her brother's wedding, his new wife started criticising her mother-in-law, saying that she didn't need her and that Matthew needed to learn how to stand up for himself against her. In Emma's opinion Maritza aspired to being rich. She said that Maritza often complained that Margaret ought to be more generous with her handouts to the family.

On 28 March 2000, the couple had their first and only child, Domenik. Maritza was thirty-six and had just stopped working as a receptionist and cleaner at Matthew's salon. When Domenik was seven months old, the Horace Street house was sold for $356 000. Margaret was repaid her loan of $150 000, for the initial purchase, and $7065, for other expenses she had incurred for the property. After discharging the mortgage, there was a $140 000 profit that Matthew wanted. Margaret was loath to give her son the entire amount. She wanted him to invest at least half of it in another house. Matthew, with a wife and child to support, had decided that it was time he became master of his own destiny and resented his mother putting conditions on the use of the money.

In the last few months of 2000, Matthew developed pain in his hand. He saw a number of doctors and physiotherapists before finding Dr Penn. Penn advised him to stop work because his hand was suffering from repetitive strain injury and cutting hair was going to make it worse. Matthew tried to sub-lease his half of the salon but the terms of the lease stopped him. Eventually, at the end of the year, he closed his business and made a claim on his insurance for disability payments. He started talking with Maritza about starting a shop together or moving their family to Spain. To follow either of those plans, they needed to get some money together. Margaret refused to hand over the profits from Horace Street for Matthew to squander by moving away from her or setting up a shop when he had no experience in retail.

After a few more arguments between them in the New Year, and some tense meetings with her solicitor, Margaret eventually released the entire $140 000 from the Horace Street sale to Matthew. He signed a Deed of Release to his mother to say that he had received the money from the trust.

While the arguments were going on, Maritza, Matthew and their baby had been renting their old house from the new owners. They lived on Matthew's insurance payments of $3000 a month and started looking for a shop to rent for a boutique.

In April the couple found a shop at 1264 High Street, Armadale, a short walk from Margaret and Paul's home. It was leased to a newsagent who was happy to accept $20 000 to vacate. They paid the landlord a year's rent in advance. Just before Easter, Matthew and Maritza flew to Hong Kong to buy stock. They bought $25 000 worth of smaller sized women's clothes and returned to set up the shop. After fitting the shop with mirrors and equipment, Maritza's Imports opened its doors for trading in June 2001. Maritza spent her days there while Matthew looked after Domenik.

In August 2001, the Wales family had an argument over the sale of Pa Lord's unit in Garfield Terrace, Surfers Paradise. The argument took six months to settle.

Matthew and Maritza marked the New Year by moving into a large rented townhouse in Burke Road, Glen Iris.

By Domenik's second birthday party on 24 March 2002, the dispute over the Surfers Paradise unit was over. Matthew and his siblings had agreed to the profits from the sale going back into a trust in favour of their mother. The Wales family spent the little boy's birthday with the Pizzaros at Matthew and Maritza's home. It was the last shared family occasion the toddler was ever going to have. On 4 April 2002, his grandmother and grandfather came over for dinner for the very last time.

Part Three
Missing

Murder is terribly exhausting.

Albert Camus, The Mother in *The Misunderstanding*,
Act 1, Scene 1

CHAPTER 6

Autumn

1–4 April 2002

THE FIRST WEEK OF APRIL 2002 WAS AN ORDINARY ONE FOR the inhabitants of 40 Mercer Road, Armadale. The extraordinary thing was that it was to become the last week of their lives.

Margaret and Paul's days were punctuated with walks down to High Street for coffee and telephone calls to and from the family. Margaret called her daughters. She rang Prudence at her holiday house in Portsea, on the most expensive tip of the Mornington Peninsula. She called Emma at her holiday farm in Trentham, an hour and a half north west of Melbourne, and Sally at her beach house in Sorrento. All three women asked their mother to come and stay with them over the weekend. Margaret made the same excuse to each of them and declined the invitations saying it was too much for Paul. It was too hard to drive out of Melbourne and away from the doctors. Margaret had Paul booked into a day care centre in Malvern on Monday and she was loath to change it.

On Wednesday 3 April, Margaret called her sister, Diana Yeldham, in Sydney. Margaret was in high spirits and looking forward to the next day. She told Di, 'I am going to be a naughty girl tomorrow, I am going to play cards.'

After a chat about each other's children, Di hung up, happy that her older sister was in a good mood. Margaret had been stressed lately. Paul had become a bit of a handful for her to look after since his last two strokes. Physically he had slowed down a lot and mentally he wasn't quite there. Di thought that the dynamic of her sister's marriage had reversed. Instead of having him doting on her and fulfilling her every whim, Margaret now had to devote herself to caring for her husband.

*

Number 40 Mercer Road is one of four townhouses in a row opposite Lauriston Girls School, an exclusive private school in one of Melbourne's wealthiest suburbs. In both location and design, the row is an expensive development. The townhouses are two storeys, fashioned from beige sandstone and capped with a slate tile roof. Inside they are well appointed with deep thick carpet, long French windows and European appliances. Typical of many built in the last decade, the neo-Georgian homes are plain but stylish. Each of the townhouses is protected from the street by a double garage which is sealed by an automatic door.

Outside number 40, a security intercom graces the entrance on the street side of the wrought iron gates – at sixty-nine, Margaret Wales-King was a security conscious woman. She felt safe in Mercer Road. On both sides of the gates the clipped balls of a pair of topiary trees in terracotta urns stand like sentries. A large plane tree, one of many in an avenue of trees, casts shadows over the nature strip. The trunk of the tree is encircled with a plastic shield to protect it from harm.

Later on Wednesday evening, Margaret and Paul went into

the neighbours', the Van Hewerdins, for a meeting with the owners of the other townhouses. There was something wrong with the plaster on the wall between number 40, Margaret and Paul's house, and Mrs Rose's house at number 38. A plasterer was going to come and have a look at it. All the neighbours agreed that he could come the following Saturday – 6 April. Margaret was pleased. She was known in her family for being houseproud and she didn't like to leave things undone for long.

On the last day of their lives, Margaret and Paul woke early and spent the morning at home. The cleaner came and polished up the already tidy house. The bookkeeper came in the morning for a few hours to organise Margaret's paperwork. She had a large share portfolio and liked to keep her bookwork up to date.

A man from a local security firm came to fix the front security gate. The buzzer access had broken and, as the gate kept the house locked from the street, Margaret wanted it fixed straight away. The house hummed with the calm, smooth efficiency well-used money can bring.

At lunchtime, the Roches arrived from their house in Somers, a small seaside town a little more than an hour south of Melbourne. Fred and Janet had both known Margaret for years. Janet knew her as a girl. They went to school together at Loreto Mandeville Hall. Fred's father had been a business associate of Margaret's father. The two couples shared an accountant, a lawyer and a preference for properties on the Mornington Peninsula. Over recent years these connections had been enough to mean that the Roches and the Kings had spent many evenings together.

In the last few weeks Janet and Margaret had started playing bridge as part of a foursome of women who had lessons with a private teacher. Margaret had completed a bridge course at a bridge school in 1994 and, at Janet's insistence, had joined the other women to develop her skills in private. A little shocked at her husband's mental demise, Margaret was determined to exercise her brain as often as she could.

When he arrived, Fred Roche helped out with a computer problem. He then drove both women to Dorothy Barnett's house in Toorak for their lesson and lunch.

At 4.30 pm Fred arrived to pick the two women up. Happy and animated after a stimulating afternoon, Margaret invited her friends in for a drink. The four of them sat in the large family room that overlooked the groomed back garden. Margaret opened a bottle of white wine and passed pretzels around in a white bowl. The couples talked about their children, the share market and travels abroad. Janet and Fred were fond of trips to Asia. Margaret expressed a preference for Noosa holidays but even those, she said, were getting a little harder due to 'changed circumstances'. Margaret nodded slightly towards Paul, who was sitting quietly, lost in his own world.

Margaret's mobile phone rang. It was her youngest son, Matthew, changing the dinner arrangements. Margaret came back to the Roches saying, 'We don't have to get there until 6.45 pm.'

Margaret poured everyone another glass of wine. It was the last bottle of the dozen lot and they might as well finish it off. One of her sons-in-law, Angus Reed, had a friend who was a wine merchant and he'd promised to deliver another couple of dozen bottles that weekend.

At 6.30 pm Margaret went upstairs and changed for dinner. She went into her large walk-in wardrobe and, from among the many hangers, picked the clothes she would never take off – grey slacks, white singlet top and belt. She picked up a light woollen jumper to throw around her shoulders. Margaret put on a gold necklace and a gold chain around her wrist. Moving into the ensuite, she put on some fresh lipstick and powder and ran a brush through her hair. Once changed, Margaret turned on the bedside lamp and turned back the bed. She liked to leave the house for the evening with everything 'just so'.

The Kings and the Roches walked out the front door together. Margaret and Paul went into the garage, got into their car and backed out into the street. The Roches had stayed to wave them off. With Margaret driving and Paul waving, the automatic garage door closed behind them. The silver Mercedes glided up Mercer Road for the last time.

5–8 April 2002

Sandra Ingpen is a busy sort of lady. She is one of those energetic women who organises others. On Friday 5 April she was busy organising a new dog for Margaret Wales-King. Since Margaret and Paul's beloved miniature schnauzer, Heide, had died a month ago, Sandra had been looking for its replacement. That week she had found one through a friend who was a dog breeder. Miniature schnauzers were popular dogs for older people. Small, silky and affectionate, the puppies were always sought after and sold quickly. Sandra had rung Margaret the day before to tell her that she had a puppy for her. The machine had answered and Margaret had not rung back. Mid-afternoon, Sandra paid a visit to Mercer Road to see Margaret. The dog breeder was holding the puppy as a favour and he was getting impatient. Sandra was running out of excuses for him.

Sandra pressed the buzzer in the security gate. It could be heard in the house. There was no answer. She could see that the low nightlights lining the path from the gate to the front door were still on. That was not like Margaret. Sandra stood back from the gate and looked up to the second storey windows. The thick curtains were drawn.

Sandra walked over to talk to an elderly man who was working in the front garden of number 42. John Van Hewerdin couldn't help Sandra; he had not seen his neighbours since the body corporate meeting two nights before. Sandra drove home down High Street. Passing Maritza's shop, she thought to call Maritza's Imports on her mobile. Margaret's daughter-in-law hadn't heard from her either.

The next morning, Saturday 6 April, a plasterer arrived at the townhouse to check the faulty wall. He rang the buzzer at 8.30 am. No one was there. He went to number 42 and woke John Van Hewerdin. John put on his dressing gown and went next door again. He rang the buzzer. The house was quiet. The night-lights were still on. Puzzled, Van Hewerdin went back inside.

Later that morning, Sandra Ingpen returned to Margaret and Paul's house. Their absence was worrying her. She wanted to get the dog sorted out and off her list of things to do. She pressed the intercom and buzzed the door. Still no answer. She drove off.

Over the weekend, Margaret's daughters stayed with their husbands and children at their holiday houses. None of them heard from their mother.

By the evening of Sunday 7 April, Emma was back in Melbourne and getting anxious. She had forgotten to ring her mother that morning to confirm a breakfast arrangement and her mother had, uncharacteristically, not rung to remind her. She and James had spent the afternoon at the Melbourne Museum and the IMAX Theatre. Her mother's silence nagged her the whole time. She made James stop the car on the way home so that she could ring her mother from a public phone booth. Neither had their mobile phones with them. The answering machine picked up the call. Emma was surprised. Margaret and Paul never usually went out on a Sunday night. When she got back to the car, Emma told James that something was not right.

When she arrived home Emma's phone was ringing. Hearing a female voice leaving a message, she rushed to grab it. It's Mum, she thought, everything is all right. It wasn't Margaret. It was Sandra telling Emma that she couldn't contact her mother and had been trying to for three days. Emma got in her car and drove from her house to her mother's. It's only about ten minutes from Toorak to Armadale, but that night Emma got to her mother's in five. Nobody was home. The door was unanswered; the house gave no clues. Emma drove slowly up High Street and went to Toorak Village. Perhaps her mother, normally a creature of habit, had changed her routine and was in one of the cafes having dinner. Perhaps. Emma didn't see her.

Emma went home and rang Prue, rang Sally, rang Margaret's house again. Now she was really worried. She went to bed for a restless night's sleep.

At 8 am on Monday 8 April, Sandra Ingpen was back at Mercer Road looking for Margaret. She, too, had not been sleeping well. There was still no sign of life at the house. Sandra went to see John Van Hewerdin. The neighbour took his copy of Margaret's key and unlocked her garage door. It was empty. The alarm was not on.

At the same time, the Wales siblings were on the telephone. Emma's calls the night before had stirred them up. Sally rang Emma, Sally rang Matthew, Matthew rang Sally and Emma, and Emma rang Damian Honan, Sally's husband.

At 9.30 am Damian and Emma met at 40 Mercer Road. Damian had Sally's spare key for her mother's house in his hand. It was a busy time for that end of the street because parents were pulling into the school car park across the road to drop their children off.

A yellow taxi came to a halt in the driveway of number 40. Emma thought that someone must be home to have called a taxi and ran towards it. 'Who are you looking for?'

'Paul King,' said the driver, checking the name against a note in his hand. 'He is going to the Girrawheen Day Care Centre.'

'Mum would never forget to cancel a taxi,' Emma said to Damian. They went into the house – there was no one there. Emma, in tears, sent the taxi away.

The phone rang in the house. It was the lady from the day care centre asking where could she find Paul King.

'We don't know,' Emma cried. 'We don't know.'

Damian and Emma looked around the house. Even though Margaret was normally fastidious about cleanliness, there were some dirty wineglasses and a bowl containing pretzel crumbs on the kitchen bench. Upstairs, the bedside lamp was on and the bed turned back. The bed was unrumpled.

Paul's nail kit, something he always carried with him to keep his nails pristine, was in his dressing room. So was his overnight bag, his wallet and driver's licence. Margaret's reading glasses and mobile phone charger were in her bedroom. Her sunglasses were on the console by the bed, making Emma think that her mother must have left the house at night. Margaret's toothbrush and face creams were in their usual spots in the ensuite.

The answering machine light was blinking red. It was full of messages from the last three days – from Sandra, from Damian Wales's wife Liz in Sydney, from Emma, Prue, Sally and from Matthew.

Emma didn't have to look any further. She left the house and drove to the closest police station.

Malvern police station is a squat plain building. It sits to the left of the grander Victorian Malvern town hall near the intersection of High Street and Glenferrie Road. The police station is walking distance from Margaret and Paul's house. Emma had never been there before. The waiting room was sterile with light blue lino on the floor and a flickering fluorescent light. There was no one standing at the counter when she arrived. While she was waiting, Emma looked around. As a former interior designer, she liked things to look aesthetically pleasing. The police station foyer was anything but. Its bare walls were pitted with spots of old Blu-Tack. A few pamphlets on community services were strewn on a brown laminated table. One was called 'Security for Seniors'. It warned older citizens not to let strangers into their homes and to keep themselves secure in the street.

Constable Rebecca Jones was on day shift watch-house duties when Emma Connell came to the station. Emma told Jones that her mother and stepfather had not been in contact with anyone in the last three days and that she wanted to report them as missing. Jones had seen a few cases of missing people in Malvern. The area had a number of nursing homes and a large proportion of older residents, so it was not uncommon for people to come in and report that a relative had gone wandering. The cases usually had a happy ending with the old person being found walking, confused and lost, in the tree-lined streets of Malvern or Armadale. Something about Emma's report made Jones think that this was not going to be one of those cases.

Jones took Margaret and Paul's details from Emma and entered them into a missing persons report on the police computer system. Known as 'Leap', the system provides information to all police stations in Victoria. The central database helped other agencies, such as hospitals and ambulance services, when they needed to identify unknown patients.

Jones took some phone numbers from Emma. She rang Di Yeldham to see if she had seen her sister. Di had no news. Jones told Emma to contact the local hospitals and as many friends and family as she could. She also asked her to bring in a recent photograph of the missing couple to help the investigation.

Emma left the station and went to James's real estate office in Armadale to check how he was going with their three kids. Then she drove back to Mercer Road and met Damian again. Together they went through Margaret's phone book and compiled a list of people they could ring. Working together, they rang through the list. No one had heard from Margaret or Paul in the last few days.

Emma went through her mother's diary. Margaret kept a note of all her engagements in it. There was nothing to indicate that she or Paul were going away. The word 'Portsea' was written in for Sunday 7 April but that had been crossed through. Another entry said 'Matt's for dinner' but that looked as if it had never happened either. Margaret had written 'cancelled' through the date.

Margaret had also written in the details of her bridge lesson with Janet Roche so Emma called her. She found out that the Roches had waved goodbye to Margaret and Paul on the evening of 4 April and hadn't seen them since. Emma rang the hospitals, Paul's doctors and the man who fixed the security door. She couldn't find anything that explained where her mother and stepfather were.

In the afternoon she drove back to Malvern police station. Sergeant Judy Cousins was on duty. A kind woman with grey hair and sparkly blue eyes, she took Emma into the police station and sat with her in the sergeant's room. Emma listed all the phone calls she had made in an effort to find her mother and stepfather. Sergeant Cousins called in Sergeant Sharon McCrory and the three women went through possible destinations for the missing couple, possible reasons for their absence or other explanations for the lack of contact. After forty minutes of speculation, Sergeant McCrory had heard enough to note in her daybook later that she had 'cause for concern for the missing couple'.

Detective Senior Constable Craig Shiell came into the sergeant's room. The detective was calm and reassuring. He had worked on a few missing persons cases in his twelve years in the force. This one smelled like something different. The police officers decided to go to the missing couple's house to see if it would yield any information on their whereabouts. Before he left for the Mercer Road house, Shiell made a telephone call.

At 5.05 pm Shiell, McCrory and Detective Senior Constable Sheahan arrived at 40 Mercer Road. Emma pulled in behind them. Damian Honan was still there and Sally had arrived from Sorrento. The three police officers looked around the house. Shiell's initial observations were that there 'did not appear to be any sign of forced entry or of a struggle. Items that would have been taken for . . . overnight travel were still present at the house'.

Sally and Emma showed McCrory the wineglasses left on the bench and the pretzel crumbs. They told the police officer that it was out of character for their mother to leave the house in this state. McCrory got on her radio and called the Malvern police station. She asked for some uniformed constables to do a doorknock of the neighbours.

Meanwhile, Sally told Emma that she had called Matthew that morning and asked him to go to the house with Emma. He had said to Sally that he had too many things on that day and couldn't really get around to their mother's. Sally was cross with Matthew because she knew that Maritza's shop was closed on Mondays and that meant he was free to come and help.

Fred and Janet Roche turned up at the house. They were worried too. They each gave the police statements setting out their afternoon with the Kings the Thursday before. Emma kept calling through the numbers in her mother's telephone book while the police took the statements in the back room. So far, the Roches had been the last people to see Margaret and Paul early on Thursday evening. During a break in her telephoning, Emma heard Janet Roche tell Detective Sheahan that Margaret had said to her, 'I'm sorry I'm going to have to kick you out now because I'm expected at my daughter's home for dinner.' Emma looked across the kitchen at Sally in disbelief. All Margaret's daughters had been out of Melbourne on the night she went missing. Sally said to Emma, 'Maybe Matthew and Maritza's?' Both women ran to the telephone.

Sally called Matthew's house. She asked him whether Margaret and Paul had eaten dinner at their house last Thursday night. She nodded to Emma, *yes they had.* 'You'd better get over here right away, Matthew.' Sally hung up. The sisters were furious. They had been thinking that the last people to see Margaret and Paul had been Fred and Janet Roche just before 7 pm on Thursday evening. In fact, their own brother had seen them later that night.

Shortly after, Matthew Wales arrived at his mother's house. Sally and Emma were in the front room with the police officers when Matthew burst into the room. In her third statement to police, dated 5 June 2001, Emma described Matthew's behaviour that evening:

> He burst into the front room, his head looked like it was going to explode and I could see the veins in his neck and his body puffed up like a blowfish. He looked very emotional and asked 'What's going on?' acting as though he was surprised to see the police and acting as though he

feared the worst. He then walked himself into the corner of the room we were in and held his eyes with his fingers and let out a distraught cry and moan. He then turned and walked back to the group of us and put his hands on his hips and said, 'Right, what's happening?' As he was saying this he seemed to be hyperventilating and he also looked like he was trying to compose himself. His face was distorted. He seemed overwhelmed by the whole situation, which I thought was an absolute overreaction as no one had mentioned anything about what had happened to them. The police had not even had the chance to introduce themselves to Matthew. For all he knew, Mum and Paul could have been away for the weekend. Sally and I were not crying – we didn't look distraught and we didn't alarm him in any way.

Emma was not convinced by her brother's display of emotion. She thought his reaction was fake.

Sally and Emma questioned Matthew about what had happened at dinner last Thursday night – what they had eaten, what Margaret and Paul had been wearing, what their moods were like, what the conversation had been and what time they had left. Matthew was vague. In between the questions, he had outbursts of emotion. He put his head between his legs and howled like a baby. 'Where's my mamma? Where's my mamma? What's happened to my mamma?' When Emma kept questioning him, Matthew cried, 'It's all a blank, I can't do this now.'

Eventually, Matthew told Emma that his mother had come for dinner wearing 'a white thin skivvy, a bolero jacket and fawn trousers ... and her usual jewellery'. Matthew said that Paul had worn 'a reefer jacket with gold buttons, a checked blue shirt and jeans'. Emma called Maritza to double-check as she felt that Matthew was being very vague. Maritza told her sister-in-law that she could not remember what Margaret had been wearing. Emma didn't believe her. 'You're in fashion, Maritza – surely you would remember something?' Maritza remembered only one thing. 'Oh yes, she had on a white t-shirt sort of thing with a belt.'

Emma then asked Maritza what time her mother and Paul had left her house after dinner. Maritza answered: 'We saw them off out the front gate at about ... I can't remember. Is Matty there? Tell him to come home – I've got a headache.' Matthew's vague memory was catching.

In response to questioning by Detective Shiell, Matthew said that he and his wife had hosted a dinner for the couple which ended at about 9.45 pm. At that time, he had walked the elderly couple to their Mercedes Benz which was parked inside Matthew's driveway and had waved them off. Shiell asked Matthew for his home phone number and he said that he could not remember it. Matthew then started crying and shaking, saying, 'I can't handle this.' Sally came in and told him to leave the room. Like the careful detective he was, Shiell kept notes of Matthew's reactions in the daybook he always carried with him. Shortly after, Matthew left Mercer Road to go home and look after his son, Domenik, while Maritza slept off her migraine.

Sally and Emma went home to their families too. After they sorted out their children, they went with their husbands, Damian and James, to Prue's house. At eight o'clock, Damian Wales flew from Sydney to Melbourne on the same flight as his aunt, Di Yeldham.

Prudence Reed, formerly Wales, lived in Toorak with her husband Angus and their three young boys. On the night that Prue's mother and stepfather were reported as missing, Angus, a

property investor, flew back early from a business meeting in
Canberra to be with Prue. He arrived home to find the family in
the middle of an emergency meeting. Everyone was there except
Matthew and Maritza – Sally and Damian, Damian Wales, Di
Yeldham, Emma and James. They sat in the lounge room with
takeaway food and talked about Margaret and Paul. There were
more questions than answers. Where were they? Why hadn't
anyone heard from them? It was so uncharacteristic for Margaret,
a careful, security conscious woman, to disappear for four days.

Emma, Damian and Sally kept ringing people listed in
Margaret's address book. Mobile phones rang constantly. The
reality was starting to hit – none of Margaret's friends or family
knew where she and Paul were. Damian Wales rang Matthew's
number throughout the night. Damian wanted to get his younger
brother over to Prue's house to answer a few questions about the
dinner on Thursday night. There was no answer. Even though
Damian left messages on the answering machine, neither
Matthew nor Maritza called back. Sally and Emma told Damian
about Matthew's emotional outbursts at Mercer Road earlier that
evening and that he had gone home because Maritza had a
headache.

At 10.50 pm, Damian slipped out of the lounge room and into
the backyard. A suspicion was forming in his mind. He called
Malvern police station. He was put through to Detective Sheahan.
Damian told Sheahan that Matthew was not with the rest of the
family, who were at Prue's searching for some answers. Damian
also told Sheahan that he believed that his brother might have had
some involvement in his parents' disappearance. Damian then
asked if the police could go to Matthew's place and check up on
him as he had failed to answer the phone. Sheahan agreed to send
a divisional van around to see if Matthew was okay.

Detectives Hodgson and Nolan arrived at Matthew and Maritza's rented, neo-Georgian two-storey house in Burke Road, Glen Iris at 12.15 am on 9 April. They found the house in darkness behind a six-foot high sandstone fence and pressed the intercom at the front gate. Matthew Wales, sleepy eyed, answered the door and let the officers into his kitchen. Maritza, looking like she had just got out of bed, came downstairs and joined her husband. The police officers explained that Damian had asked them to check on him as he had failed to answer his phone. Matthew said that he had taken a Panadeine Forte and fallen asleep. He also told the detectives: 'I'm just a bit upset and concerned about my mother, you know.'

Detective Hodgson did not know, he was not convinced. He wrote in his notebook at the time that: 'Matthew Wales didn't appear to be sincere when he said this and at no time did he mention his father.'

Back at Prue's house, Emma too had her suspicions. Although it had been a long hard day, her mind was still racing trying to put the pieces together. When Matthew finally arrived at Prue's in the early hours of Tuesday 9 April, he started crying and howling again. 'Where's my mamma?'

Emma was unmoved. She said later: 'Unfortunately I could show him no affection because, really, I smelled a rat.' Emma found it surprising and disappointing that Maritza had not called any of her sisters-in-law to express her concern or sympathy or to find out whether there had been any developments.

While the Wales siblings were gathered at Prue's house, the three detectives at the Malvern police station Criminal Investigation Unit had been busy. Sheahan and McCrory had conducted a doorknock of the neighbouring houses in Mercer Road that had led to the discovery of the Wales-King gardener,

Giuseppe Vercellino. Vercellino confirmed that he had tended Margaret and Paul's garden on Friday 5 April but had not seen his employers.

Other neighbours told Sheahan of the Wednesday night body corporate meeting about the state of the wall. No one in the area had seen the couple since the morning of 4 April.

Sharon McCrory organised a broadcast over the police radio describing the missing couple and their car. She faxed the missing persons report to Trentham and Sorrento police stations because Emma, Sally and Prue had holiday homes in those areas. She also contacted the Rosebud and Frankston hospitals, the closest to the Mornington Peninsula, to see if anyone meeting the descriptions of Margaret and Paul had been admitted.

At 10 pm McCrory sent a young constable to the townhouse at 40 Mercer Road to keep it secure and keep watch. Margaret and Paul's stylish home had officially become a crime scene.

In the room next to Sergeant McCrory, Detective Shiell looked at his notes. The telephone call he had made before going to the Mercer Road house was to the ANZ bank where Margaret Wales-King and Paul King held a number of accounts. Since he had been out of the station, a response from the bank had come in. The detective bristled with alarm – the couple's substantial bank accounts had not been touched since 3 April 2002.

Detective Shiell picked up the telephone and dialled the Homicide Squad's number. The missing persons case of Margaret Wales-King and Paul King was less than a day old and had already changed its character. It was now a suspected murder.

CHAPTER 7

Hiding

5 April 2002

WHEN DAYLIGHT POKED THROUGH THE CLOUDS ON FRIDAY 5 April, Matthew and Maritza were still wide awake. They hadn't slept at all. They had lain in bed and talked. Matthew tried to calm Maritza down. She was panicking and begged him to call the police and tell them what he had done. Matthew pleaded with his wife to give him some more time before he did anything. He tried to explain to her that once he had killed his mother and step-father he felt freer than he had been for ages. He wanted to stay, feeling like that, with Maritza and Domenik for a while longer.

Matthew had been up and down all night checking on the bodies. He had looked out of the bedroom window at them lying on his front lawn. He thought he heard noises. He went downstairs to check. He came back and climbed into bed. He was so cold. His face was white and sweating. He started crying. 'Oh, Maritza, Maritza. Do you still love me?' Over and over again.

She answered his question with one of her own. 'What are you going to do?'

'I'll fix it.'

It was barely light when Matthew dressed and went down to the bodies again. He had a pea-green sheet from the linen cupboard in his hand. Under the pool, his mother's face had frozen in a bloodied grimace. He didn't want to look at her or Paul anymore. He ripped the sheet in half and wrapped a piece of cloth around each face. He firmly knotted the cloth under the chin of each body, covering their expressions. He dragged Domenik's pool back over the bodies.

At 7 am Matthew left the house and drove to the National Australia Bank automatic teller machine at the Tooronga Village shops. He took out some cash. There were a few things he needed to buy.

Just up the road from Matthew's house there was a Mobil service station which opened early and had small trailers for hire. Matthew was the second customer that morning to hire a box trailer. He filled out the hire form using his real name and his old Horace Street address. He also bought a D-shaped metal shackle to connect the trailer to the car. He didn't really have a plan but he knew he had to get rid of the bodies from his front lawn. All he wanted to do was have a normal life with Maritza and Domenik and to do that he had to make sure the bodies weren't found.

Matthew handed the guy behind the counter his bank keycard to pay for the trailer hire. The trailer was quite light and flimsy but it would do the job. Matthew hooked it up to the Nissan Patrol and drove home.

Matthew unhooked the trailer and pushed it onto the lawn next to the pool-covered mound. He saw Domenik's little face pressed up to the window in the toy room, watching him. Matthew went inside the house to make him breakfast.

Maritza was up too. She was a mess, her eyes red raw from a

night of crying. She wouldn't let him touch her. He told her to go to work like she normally did. She was too distraught to stay at home. Perhaps getting her out of the house might help her concentrate on other things and relax a bit. Once Domenik was settled in front of the television, Matthew grabbed Maritza by the arms and pulled her close to him. He looked down into her face. 'Just forget about this at the moment. There's nothing else we can do. I will speak to the police when I am ready. I want to spend some more time with you and Dom.' Maritza pulled out of his grasp and turned away, refusing to look at him.

Before Maritza took the car to the shop, Matthew drove to t he local hardware store, Tait Timber and Hardware. He bought five metres of red and white striped sash cord, six one-metre lengths of thick stainless steel chain and five more 'D' shackles. Waiting in the queue with all the other men, Matthew could almost persuade himself it was a normal day and he had some handyman jobs to do. Almost – until he thought of his mother and stepfather lying on the front lawn. He never would be just one of the other guys.

Across the road from Tait's was the Melbourne Brick Company. Matthew saw an assistant in the front yard serving two men in dirty blue overalls. He interrupted them and asked if he could buy some concrete bricks. He told the assistant that he needed the bricks for a feature in a fireplace he was building at home. The man told Matthew that concrete bricks wouldn't work for that sort of job because the fire's heat would shatter the concrete. He said to try pressed clay bricks.

Matthew found himself getting angry. He told the assistant that he knew exactly what he wanted – concrete bricks about two feet long and eight inches high. The man turned back to his other customers, telling Matthew to help himself to a pile of grey concrete bricks that were left over from a display wall. Matthew carried three bricks, which had holes drilled through their middles, back to his car.

When he got home, Maritza left for the shop. Matthew spent the morning keeping Domenik amused and inside. He didn't want his son lifting up the pool on the front lawn.

By noon, Domenik was asleep again. Matthew put on a pair of latex gloves from the box in the kitchen. He found two folded, clean double quilt covers in the linen cupboard. He took them outside. There was nobody in the window of the flat across the road. Matthew pulled the pool off the bodies. His mother's hooded body was stiff as wood and just as heavy. He could feel the chill of her skin through his glove. Matthew lifted her awkwardly and slid her inside a lime green checked quilt cover. Paul's body was a bit smaller but just as cold and rigid. Matthew dragged a blue cotton cover over him.

Once the bodies were lying inside their envelopes of cotton, Matthew tucked the fabric around them. He took the sash cord and, winding it around each body in an oblique spiral, pulled the material tight. He tied a heavy length of chain around his step-father's neck and then across his body. He threaded another length of chain through the three square concrete bricks and connected it with the 'D' shackles. Despite the scattered chatter of his mind, Matthew thought perhaps he would put the bodies into some water, a dam somewhere. The last thing he wanted was them bobbing up to the surface. The efforts of the morning and the night before caught up with him and Matthew went inside, leaving the wrapped bodies on the grass.

Nervously, Matthew called Maritza at the shop again. He had called her every half-hour or so throughout the day. He wanted to make sure she was okay and that she had stopped panicking. He told her that he was starting to get a bit emotional and that he looked at Domenik and just wanted to cry. He asked Maritza to come home. She didn't really want to talk to him.

Matthew went back to the bodies on the front lawn. At the head end of each body, blood had seeped through the doona covers onto the grass. Using the rope and chain wrapped around them to get a grip, Matthew hefted his mother and stepfather up onto the floor of the trailer and lay them head-to-toe alongside each other. He put the pool back over them and added some old paint tins and a sawhorse so that the mound looked like a pile of rubbish. He pulled a blue tarpaulin over the load and tied it at the four corners of the trailer. Rolling the laden trailer into the garage, Matthew went inside to wake his son.

Maritza came home from work early. Despite the usual Friday afternoon busyness of High Street, she had done little trade. She was too stressed to turn on the charm so few customers had been persuaded to buy anything. When she got home, Matthew told her not to go into the garage. 'I've still got them in the trailer.'

That night, lying in their bed, Maritza and Matthew talked for hours in the dark. Maritza cried a bit more but was calmer than she had been the night before. A day of taking strong migraine tablets had taken the edge off her nerves and drugged her senses a little. She pleaded with Matthew to ring the police, to make it right and sort out the mess he had gotten them into. She was scared that the police would take Domenik from them once they found out what Matthew had done.

Matthew cried too. He wanted more time to think it all through. He told Maritza over and over again that all that mattered was that he had some normal time with her and Dom before the police caught him. He was surprised they hadn't come knocking on his door already. 'Maybe,' he told Maritza, 'the woman across the road didn't see me kill them.' Maybe he would get his normal life after all.

6 April 2002

On Saturday morning, Maritza went to work again. She couldn't wait to leave the house. Matthew dropped Domenik and Maritza in High Street just before 10 am. By 10.09 am, he was at Dean's True Value Hardware in Malvern Road using his credit card to buy a mattock and a big bottle of Liquid Magnet, an industrial cleaner for cement surfaces.

At 10.19 am, Matthew was at Fulton's Garden Supplies in East Malvern where he ordered half a metre of Surecrop compost to be delivered on Monday 8 April between 8 am and 8.30 am. Matthew used his credit card to pay the $60 fee. He drove home and hooked the trailer up to the car.

By mid-morning Maritza was sick in the stomach and could feel a flickering of lights behind her eyes, warning that a migraine was coming. At lunchtime it was clear that she wasn't going to get through the day. She rang Matthew and told him to come and get her. He brought her new prescription migraine tablets with him. Once home, Maritza started vomiting. Drowsy with the medication, she went straight upstairs to bed.

Matthew put Domenik to bed. At 12.38 pm he made a telephone call to his mother's house. Her voice on the answering machine gave him a jolt. He left a message anyway, asking Margaret for some information about Maritza's new migraine tablets. He thought it might be useful, later, if a message from him on that day was found on her machine.

Driving with the trailer bumping behind him, Matthew headed to Burwood Road to the Hartwell BP service station, up the road from Glen Iris. He filled up the car with twenty dollars worth of fuel. He went into the shop to pay for the petrol and buy a map with his credit card. He thought that he would keep his cash for any purchases he might need to make out of the city. As he was waiting to pay, Matthew watched the laden trailer in the service station's driveway.

Matthew got back into the car and drove through the eastern suburbs to the Maroondah Highway. On the passenger seat beside him were black rubbish bags. Into one Matthew had put his mother's car keys and Louis Vuitton handbag. He and Maritza had bought it for her the Easter before last while on a buying trip to Hong Kong. They had thought Margaret would prefer chocolate brown leather to an Easter egg. Another bag held the jumper his mother had worn, slung around her shoulders, to dinner. Margaret's gold earrings, thick gold necklace, a gold bracelet and a plain gold ring were thrown in another bag. Matthew had taken the jewellery off his mother's body so that, if she were found, it would look like a robbery. He hadn't taken it all off, though – three diamond rings were left on her finger. Before leaving, Matthew had broken his mother's mobile phone in half and thrown it in the bin outside his house. In the last bag, he had thrown his mother and stepfather's shoes together with the bloodstained blue tracksuit and slippers he had worn on Thursday night.

Matthew drove without any real thought as to where he was heading. He made a few stops to dump the plastic bags into public bins in shopping strips that were close to the road. He could feel the weight of the trailer pulling on the back of his car. Every time he looked in his rear vision mirror, he saw the blue plastic mound with the sawhorse on top in the trailer. The image of the bloodied bundles under the tarp stayed in his mind as he drove. He was worried the tarp might lift up in the wind. Checking in the mirror again, he wouldn't have been surprised to see his mother sitting up, stiff in death, her face streaked with blood.

When he got to Bunnings Hardware store in Croydon, one of the last of the eastern suburbs before the scenery turned bucolic, Matthew stopped to buy a crowbar and a *Guide to Garden Ponds*. Waiting in the line to pay, Matthew glanced down at the label stuck to the handle of the crowbar. He'd chosen a 'Mumme' product – the label bore a picture of a bandaged man. Matthew paid by Visa card and left the store. He ran back to his car and the trailer.

Matthew had no destination in mind but simply a vague impression that he should head for the bush. His mother had loved the country and at least he could leave her someplace she would have liked.

After driving for three hours and taking a few wrong turns, Matthew was pleased to find a dirt track that ran off the road to Warburton, a pretty country town, and wound into the depths of the National Park. The trees were dense and closely planted leaving little room for light or human settlement. He drove into the bush, got out of the car and walked. It was a quiet place, the few cars travelling past on the road could be heard for minutes before coming into sight. The main sound was the wind whistling through the trees as it came up the hill. About twenty metres from the car, he discovered a small area of ground that was free of trees. Matthew had found a place desolate enough to bury his mother and stepfather.

He picked up the mattock and started to dig. The loamy soil gave way easily and soon he had cut a large rectangle in the ground. He shovelled the soft soil away and dug until the hole was the length of his mother and a bit wider. Once the hole was long enough, Matthew concentrated on making it deeper. After a couple of hours, it was hard to swing the mattock properly so he used the crowbar. He swung it above his head and down into the dirt over and over again, until his muscles strained and hurt.

By six o'clock, Matthew Wales was in the middle of nowhere, in the dark of the forest with the two bodies beside him. He started hearing noises, to his left, to his right and then straight in front of him. It was so dark, but he didn't want to put the parking lights on in case they attracted attention. He was more scared than he had ever been in his life. He just wanted to get out of there. He was beginning to regret ever getting himself into this situation.

After another two hours of digging, a metallic ping rang out into the forest as the crowbar hit rock. It was time to stop. Matthew dragged the bodies off the trailer. He pushed his mother into the bottom of the grave and then rolled Paul in. If they are going to stay here, he thought, at least Paul gets to be on top for once. Whatever he thought about Paul and what Paul had done to him, the man had loved his mother unconditionally and had received little reward for his devotion.

Matthew put Domenik's pool over Paul and then threw in the three concrete bricks threaded onto the chain. He shovelled the soft soil back into the grave. Once the hole was filled in, there was a pile of extra soil left over. He shaped it into a small mound which he then pounded flat with his feet.

After the longest afternoon of his life, Matthew climbed back into his car and drove out of the forest. As he reached the inter-section where the dirt road met the sealed road back to Melbourne, a white four-wheel drive with two men in it came around the bend. Matthew hadn't seen or heard anyone for hours and was not expecting any cars on the road. He slammed his brakes on and pulled his baseball cap lower over his eyes. Matthew's heart thudded in his chest as the car passed.

Coming into Camberwell, Matthew threw the crowbar out the window onto a neat nature strip. The empty trailer bounced around behind him as pulled into his driveway.

Maritza was still drowsy when her husband arrived home. She didn't ask him where he had been and he didn't volunteer anything. She didn't want to know.

CHAPTER 8

Hunting

6 April 2002

ON THE FIRST FRIDAY IN APRIL, JAMIE TONKIN AND CRAIG Lamont were men on a mission. Both Yarra Valley locals and devoted deer hunters, they drove to the Stalkers' Camp at the Thompson Jordan Divide to see if there were any signs of deer. The Divide, known by locals as TJ, is in an area on Woods Point Road where the road runs like a river through two large forests – Big River Forest to the north and Yarra Ranges National Park to the south. The camp was a good 37 kilometres into the forest east of Cumberland Junction and was far enough from everything and everybody to get some good hunting done. Not too many sight-seers or daytrippers made their way to the area. It was not a convenient place for aimless wandering. Most people who travelled that far into the forest had some reason for being there.

Tonkin and Lamont arrived at the camp in the late afternoon of 5 April and set up a fire. Stalking was an ancient form of hunting deer – all you needed was a gun and a pair of feet. The fancier hound hunting was due to start the next weekend so the men thought they'd get a good look at the deer before the hounds came running through and scared them off.

To get to TJ, the hunters took Lamont's Landcruiser down Woods Point Road. Since he was a kid, Tonkin had been up and down that road hundreds of times to go camping, fishing or deer hunting. While working with Lamont at a nursery, Tonkin had shared his love of deer hunting with his friend. Seven years later, the two men had clocked up over two hundred hunting trips in the Yarra Ranges National Park and the Thompson State Forest.

The men got up early on Saturday 6 April and had a few good hours stalking down in the gullies. They found a couple of large deer wallows, marks in the mud caused by stags rolling around to mark their territory, and some more signs of deer downstream. By lunchtime the hunters had only seen one deer, off in the distance where the land got too steep to climb. Tired and hungry, they went back to camp. They got the fire going and had a feed of eggs and oysters, coffee and beer. The afternoon turned hot. Tonkin and Lamont were getting worried about snakes so they decided to pack up the guns and finish hunting for the day. For a while, the talk turned to going fishing but as the beer did its work, the men decided to go home.

Lamont was driving his Landcruiser down Woods Point Road towards Cumberland Junction. He and Tonkin were trying to out-brag each other about the size of deer they had shot when a red Nissan Patrol braked suddenly on a track on their left.

Tonkin had a good look at the Nissan, not only because his wife was a petrol-head and some of it had worn off on him, but because it was pulling a trailer. He thought the driver had a deer in it. What's more, Tonkin thought, if he's come out of that track (which goes to the Upper Yarra Dam catchment area) then that's an illegally shot deer in there. Tonkin knew that you had to have authorisation to go into the catchment area and the Nissan didn't look like a National Parks car. Lamont and Tonkin chuckled.

They reckoned the driver thought that, in the white four-wheel drive, they were rangers and was panicking. He sure had slammed on his brakes when he saw them coming.

Tonkin remembered later that the Nissan was in good nick. Unlike lots of other four-wheel drives in the area, it was clean and undented. A real 'Toorak tractor'. From what Tonkin could see the trailer didn't seem to have any deer in it, it was small and covered with a cheap blue tarpaulin of the sort sold by variety stores. No lumps of firewood stuck out of the trailer and there was no sign of a motorbike. The tarp was tied down on three of its four corners. The fourth corner was flapping in the wind. It looked like the trailer was empty.

The hunters continued home. The red Nissan went its own way.

CHAPTER 9

Panicking

7 April 2002

EARLY THE NEXT MORNING MATTHEW WALES WAS DIGGING again. This time it was the grass in his front yard. He dug a garden bed out of the lawn and put the slabs of grass and soil into the trailer. Maritza came out and asked him what he was doing.

'I'm just making a garden bed.'

'Why now?'

'I'm putting dirt on the trailer because I have to go back. They need . . . they need some more dirt.' Maritza didn't ask him any more questions.

Matthew kept digging until he had cut out a rectangle of grass from the place where his mother and stepfather had lain. He wanted to remove any signs that they had been there. After the grass was out, he dug the soil up in preparation for the delivery of compost the next morning.

Maritza took Domenik to pick up her nephew James's birthday cake. He was having a party and ages ago, before the nightmare had started, she had promised her sister, Patricia, that she would collect the cake from Noble Park, on the other side of town.

While Maritza and Domenik were out, Matthew used the

whole bottle of Liquid Magnet to scrub the grey paving stones outside the front door and the floor of the garage. There were two bloodstains on the paving marking the place where Margaret and Paul had first fallen. He took everything out of the garage and cleaned it with the high-pressure hose. Although Matthew couldn't see her, the woman who lived across the road above the wine shop was watching his cleaning frenzy and would remark upon it later to police.

When Maritza got home she put Domenik to bed. When he woke, the three of them went to the party. It was the first contact they had had with anyone since the murders and it was hard to keep up appearances. The Pizzaro family were all there – Maritza's parents, her brother Mario and his partner, her sister and brother-in-law and their children. James was very excited and everyone was in a good mood. Everyone except Maritza and Matthew. They both struggled through the afternoon, trying to appear normal.

When they went to bed that night, Maritza started crying again. She was upset that she couldn't tell her sister what was happening. She was close to Patricia and usually told her every-thing. Now she had to avoid being alone with her in case she found herself blurting out what Matthew had done.

Matthew was wrung out too. He cried with her. Maritza held him.

'What is going to happen? What's going to happen to us? What's going to happen to Dom?'

Matthew reassured his wife. 'They will never be found.'

As they lay in bed crying, the phone rang downstairs. The call went straight onto the answering machine. It was Sally Honan, Matthew's eldest sister, ringing to see if Matthew knew where their mother was. The sisters were getting worried. No one had seen or heard from Margaret and Paul for days.

8 April 2002

On Monday morning Matthew was up early again. Fultons had delivered the compost and he wanted to dig it into the new garden bed.

He rang Sally back. She told him that she was trying to find their mum. 'Do you know where she is?'

'I have no idea.' The lying had begun.

'Well, I'm still at the beach. Could you go with Emma to the house?'

'Yes, okay.'

Matthew had no intention of going to his mother's house but he couldn't tell his sister that. He rang his other sister, Emma, instead.

'Emma, I can't go to Mum's. Can you get Damian to go with you? Sally has the spare key. I've got a few things to do.'

The thing Matthew had to do was to cover the grave of his mother and stepfather with more soil from his garden. If he didn't do that, wild animals might dig up the bodies. Maritza had the day off. The shop was shut on Mondays and she was going to stay home with Domenik.

Matthew left the house early in the morning, pulling the trailer of grass and dirt behind him. This time Matthew's journey was much quicker. He had memorised the route to the forest and, unlike the first visit, didn't waste any time making wrong turns. He made two stops on the way to buy petrol and river rocks. Banksia Garden Supplies was not far from where he used to have his hairdressing salon, Hairhouse Warehouse, in Knox City Shopping Centre. He had been there often to buy things for the garden of his old house. This visit he bought six large river rocks and a ball of green bailing twine to tie the tarp down over the trailer.

Once he passed Marysville, Matthew followed the road to Cambarville he had taken two days earlier. On his first visit he had measured the distance so that he would be able to find the grave site again. He knew he had 26 kilometres to go before he was near the dirt track. Finally, the small red triangle that marked the track appeared. Matthew pulled into the bush near the grave. He was surprised to find that the pile of earth he had stamped down was undisturbed. Using a rake and shovel he had brought from home, Matthew covered the rectangle of bare soil with the grass from his lawn and the river rocks. Hopefully the grass would grow over the rocks and make it look natural. He considered cutting down a few of the smaller trees nearby to strew them over the grave and then thought better of it. After all, it was a pretty remote area and he was keen to get home.

Coming back into the suburbs of Melbourne, Matthew stopped at a car spa and cleaned the car and trailer with their brushes and hoses. He threw the map and the tarp into the spa's bin.

At 3.00 pm Matthew returned the trailer. As he pulled into his driveway, he realised that it was an unseasonably warm day and that he felt lighter than he had done for ages.

Late in the afternoon, Sally rang from their mother's house. She was furious with him. 'Did Mum and Paul have dinner at your house on Thursday night?'

'Yes, they did.' There was no point lying about that.

'Matthew, we've all been looking for them. Get your arse over here straight away.'

Matthew drove to 40 Mercer Road, Armadale. The lights were on. Two police cars and his sisters' cars were parked out the front. It was time to face the family.

CHAPTER 10

Investigating

9 April 2002

AT 8.45 AM ON TUESDAY 9 APRIL, DETECTIVE SERGEANT HENRY Van Veenendaal and Detective Senior Constable Narelle Fraser of the Homicide Squad arrived at the Malvern Criminal Investigation Unit in Glenferrie Road. The two detectives were under the command of Detective Sergeant Steve Waddell and were part of the crew of six assigned to the suspected homicides of Margaret Wales-King and Paul King. On the first morning of the investigation, Detective Senior Constable Shiell told the Homicide detectives what he knew so far, including the fact that the elderly couple had not accessed their money for five days.

In every homicide investigation, the police officers working on it have been trained to maintain an impartial view of events and to approach every piece of information as a possible lead that may solve the case one way or the other. Hanging in every police station in Victoria is the force's code of ethics: 'I uphold the right in my role within the Victoria Police Force by acting impartially

with integrity and by providing service excellence to everyone.'
The Homicide Squad prides itself on upholding the code to the
highest degree when they are investigating a suspicious death.
The squad's detectives must go thoroughly down any path to
which information leads them even if simply to determine that it
was a dead end. When investigating a case, all detectives are
mindful of the fact that they may end up in a court giving evidence about the steps they took to solve it.

Once a case is opened and a crew assigned, it is christened with
an operational codename. There is an office within the Victoria
Police whose sole purpose is to name operations. Codenames
cannot be picked at random. They must be selected by the codename office and then passed through a chain of command for
approval. After an investigation of a one-eyed criminal was christened Operation Cyclops, a guideline was introduced prohibiting
offensive codenames. The Wales-King missing persons case
became a homicide investigation with the nondescript name of
Operation Compradore.

Each operation has an analyst appointed to it who acts as a central gathering point and filter of all the information found.
Operation Compradore's analyst was Senior Constable Helen
Nugent. Nugent's training at the Victoria Police Detective
Training School was put to the test in April and May 2002, when
she worked through the enormous amount of information given
to her about the Wales-King case. Every officer working on the
investigation kept a series of information reports which detailed
any inquiries they made and the results. The reports were for-
warded to Nugent. After the media became involved in the case,
the Victoria Police Crime Stoppers telephone call service was
swamped with more than 1800 calls. Despite the fact that most
of them were of no use whatsoever, a small number of calls

contained nuggets of significant information. To keep track of all the threads of the story, Nugent entered the information reports into her computer. She worked out which pieces were useful and which were not and passed her observations on to Waddell.

Very early in the investigation, Nugent had the telephone numbers of Margaret and Paul's families, a record of their recent calls in and out and details of their social and financial lives. On the streets of Melbourne's more affluent suburbs, uniformed police and plain clothes detectives were using Nugent's data as a compass for finding out all they could about the missing couple's lives. Details of where they went, who they went with and what they did when they got there, were all gathered and fed into Nugent's database.

Another initial step in any murder investigation is to check all points of departure for passengers matching the missing persons. Full descriptions and a photograph of Margaret and Paul were shown to staff at every air and sea port and major railway station in Australia. The hundreds of city and country bus companies whose vehicles crisscross the country provided passenger lists which were checked for travellers matching the missing couple's description. In the middle of one of the first of many 18-hour shifts on the case, the Compradore crew were combing through the passenger lists faxed to the Homicide Squad's offices. They had been at it for hours and not seen anything interesting when suddenly one entry jumped out. On a list of people travelling from Townsville to Ingham in the north of Queensland was a booking for 'P. King and female' for 5 April 2002. Next to the booking details was a mobile telephone number. Thousands of kilometres away, Paul King, jackaroo, got the surprise of his life when the Homicide Squad detectives called him. Pleasant as he was, he couldn't help them.

Just after the Homicide officers finished the handover meeting, the Wales sisters and their brother Damian arrived at the Malvern police station for a briefing. Neither Matthew nor Maritza joined them.

The police wanted to find out as much as they could about the missing couple from Margaret's children. Each of them would be asked to provide a statement. The Wales sisters were very keen to help and had a lot of information about the couple's personalities and social life to share with police. It quickly became apparent that first morning that neither the sisters nor Damian Wales knew much about their mother's financial position.

At 10.50 am Detectives Van Veenendaal, Shiell and Fraser went with the family back to Mercer Road. Senior Constables Peter Cox and Stephen Lake from the Crime Scene Unit of the Victorian Forensic Science Centre were already at the house conducting forensic examinations. The two units working at the house left each other alone. They had different reasons for being there. The Homicide Squad detectives were looking at the house for some clues as to the sort of people Margaret Wales-King and Paul King were, what sort of lives they lived and what would take them away from the comfort of Mercer Road.

In contrast, the crime scene examiners were focusing on the little details. On arrival at a crime scene, they always follow the same protocol. Before touching anything, the examiners seal the scene and prevent any material being taken out without it being recorded in a crime scene logbook. Next they visually record the scene, as it is found, by sketching it, photographing it and, in some cases, videoing it. After the original scene is recorded, the examiners start moving things and searching for forensic material, footprints or shoe impressions, fingerprints, fingernail clippings or hairs, traces of DNA in sweat or blood or fibres that look like they came from somewhere else – anything that may assist the investigation. Forensic science is based on the theory that every contact leaves a trace. It is the job of the Crime Scene Unit, and the forensic scientists at the Victorian Forensic Science Centre who analyse the material, to find the traces and identify them. The investigating officers then use the information gathered from the traces to find a suspect.

No signs of violence were found in the search of 40 Mercer Road on the first day of the investigation. Whatever had happened to its occupants had probably happened somewhere else. The house did hold some clues, though, for those trained to observe them. When the Homicide detectives looked around Margaret and Paul's house, they saw glasses in the sink and pretzel crumbs in the bowl on the bench. Margaret's daughters were adamant that their mother would never have left her home like that voluntarily. The officers also found the couple's bed turned back, the bedside lamp on and overnight bags in their wardrobes. They noticed that Margaret and Paul had left without taking her prescription sunglasses, his medication or the mobile phone charger. From what the daughters were saying, Margaret would have packed carefully for any overnight trip.

The downstairs answering machine was full of unanswered messages. Shiell took a copy of the tape as evidence. The house had a security alarm with the details of its provider written on a sticker on the front. Van Veenendaal rang the alarm company. He was told that the house alarm had not been activated since about 15 March and had certainly not been used in the last five days.

Waddell arrived at the house just after 11 am and was briefed by the other detectives. Waddell then introduced himself as head of the Homicide Squad's Missing Persons Unit to Emma, Prue, Sally and Damian. He told them that the morning's search of their mother's house had not revealed any signs of forced entry, robbery or violence.

At 11.25 am, Mercer Road received another visitor. Matthew Wales arrived with a handwritten note in which he had set out the details of the conversation he had with his mother and stepfather during the dinner at his house on the evening of 4 April. Waddell read it, but Matthew's notes didn't help him.

At lunchtime, Van Veenendaal and Fraser started a door-knock of Margaret and Paul's neighbours and Shiell walked south down Mercer Road to High Street. Where the two streets meet there is an antique centre, a bespoke jeweller and a white-gloved removalist's office. In an area consumed with moving up in all its forms, High Street, Armadale is a strip shopping centre in which it is impossible to buy a tomato or a litre of milk. Nearly all the shops in High Street sell items of decoration for the house, the face or the body. Designer clothes, French face creams, Persian rugs, antiques and original fine art are displayed for the picking by those with enough money or credit to do so. Bridal parties make special trips to the area to order tailor-made dresses. The shops in High Street don't satisfy themselves with selling products alone – they aim to purvey an accompanying lifestyle. Shopkeepers hand out philosophies on the back of their business cards. Observations such as 'Have nothing in your homes that you do not know to be useful or believe to be beautiful' or 'Without hats, an intrinsic part of fashion, we would have no civilisation' come for free.

Seeking her own part of the High Street culture, Maritza Wales, Chilean-born and Boronia-bred, had set up Maritza's Imports, specialising in European designer clothes for women. Trying to establish a clientele amongst the wealthy, eastern sub-urbs women for whom shopping is a vocation, Matthew and Maritza bought stock aimed at the skinny, expensive end of the market. Perhaps for this reason, the shop was not really the financial success they had hoped it would be. At the time Margaret and Paul disappeared, business expenses outweighed the profits to the tune of $52 000. After nine months of trading, the shop's customer traffic had slowed down to an unviable level.

Maritza had worked in retail before, selling ladies clothes at a Myer's department store and shoes in Collins Street, but this was the first business she had owned. While Matthew had run his hairdressing salon successfully he knew little about women's clothes. Recently, Maritza and Matthew had put Maritza's Imports on the market and were talking about opening a coffee shop. For the time being, Maritza was still behind the counter at 1264 High Street, Armadale and that was where Shiell found her at noon on 9 April. Even though it was lunchtime, and the women outside were pounding the footpath in well-heeled shoes, Maritza's Imports was sufficiently untroubled by customers that its proprietor had time to provide a five-page statement to the detective.

In her statement, Maritza described the evening of 4 April and her in-laws' visit. She told Shiell that they had eaten vegetarian risotto for dinner and drunk two bottles of wine. She said that her in-laws had played with Domenik and looked through Maritza and Matthew's wedding photographs. The evening had finished with cups of chamomile tea sweetened with honey and Matthew, Maritza and Domenik waving goodbye at 9.45 pm. Maritza said that she thought her in-laws had driven home. She said that Matthew did not leave the house after dinner that night or make any telephone calls.

Maritza also described the history of her relationship with Matthew and his family. She said that the Wales family 'has always had its ups and downs but everyone got along fine. Mum was sometimes a bit standoffish. She was a bit snobby. She never mentioned to me having any problems or fights with anyone else. Matthew and I have never had any problems with the other sons and daughters.'

In response to a question from Shiell about their financial position, Maritza told him: 'We have never had any problems with drugs or gambling or debts. Matthew has never spoken about owing people money apart from bills.'

An hour or so later, Shiell had to go back to Maritza's shop to ask her what the missing couple had been wearing when they came for dinner. Although Maritza was not expecting Shiell to return, she had the same calm demeanour during the second, unannounced visit that she had displayed during the first. The detective didn't notice anything unusual about her.

About the same time that Maritza was receiving her second visit from Shiell, Matthew was at the Malvern police station providing a five-page statement to Detective Senior Sergeant Waddell. Matthew's account of the evening of 4 April was similar to his wife's. He told Waddell that his guests remained at his home until about 9.45 to 10 pm. He said that when his mother and stepfather left, Matthew, Domenik and Maritza went outside to see them off:

Mum continued to talk about gardening and garden design. She picked up the hose and started to flick it about, she likes to water the garden. When they left Mum drove and although they didn't say where they were going I assumed that they were going home. They reversed out of my driveway and drove off towards Wattletree Road ... I did not hear from either Mum or Paul again that night and I have not seen either of them since that time.

He could not provide the detective with any explanation for the couple's disappearance: 'Their disappearance is totally out of character. I am not aware of any problems that they may have been having and as I stated when I last saw them they appeared to be their normal selves.'

When asked about his sisters' calls to him to trace his parents' last movements, Matthew could not remember any details. 'I am a bit vague at the moment and I feel a bit dizzy because I have taken something for my nerves. I think it is an anti-anxiety tablet that my brother-in-law Angus gave to me just before I came to the police station.'

During the day, police took statements from two more of Margaret Wales-King's children – Emma Connell and Damian Wales. Emma Connell provided Detective Senior Constable Narelle Fraser with a seven-page account of her family history and the events of the last few days. During the investigation, Emma kept many foolscap notepads full of extensive notes of the steps she had taken, the conversations she had and the observations she made. In the first of four statements, she told Fraser that: 'To my knowledge Mum and Paul have no enemies and no reason for anyone to want to harm them. This is absolutely and totally out of character.' She described her family as a 'very close family' noting that there hadn't been many times when the four Melbourne-based children did not live near each other.

Damian Wales lives in Sydney and had come to Melbourne the day before his interview with police, so he had less to say than his sister about the search for his mother and stepfather. He did tell Detective Sergeant McInnis that he didn't know of any person who had a grudge against his mother or Paul. He described his mother as 'very forthright with people as well as charming'. Paul was a 'very conservative person'.

By the end of the first day of the investigation, the detectives had taken four statements, knocked on many doors and made scores of telephone calls. It was time to get the media involved.

10 April 2002

The next morning, Detective Inspector Brian Rix, the head of the Homicide Squad, asked the family to participate in a media release. Little did he or the Wales siblings know what effect the media involvement would have on the case or, for the family, their lives. The Wales-King case was to become one of the most publicised homicide operations in Australia's history. Eventually the Victoria Police Media Liaison Unit would be so besieged by media requests about the case that it refused to speak about it. On 10 April, however, giving a media conference seemed the logical thing to do.

Police media conferences take place in a specially built room of the Victoria Police Centre in the World Trade Centre building, a large sandstone complex that perches on the banks of the Yarra River at the south-western edge of the city. The media are invited to the police media conference and the case is introduced by a high ranking officer, like Inspector Rix, who do a 'stand up' interview outlining the facts of the investigation so far. This is followed by an appeal from members of the victims' family for assistance in finding their loved ones.

Inspector Rix told the gathered media that Margaret Wales-King and Paul King 'are people you wouldn't class as at risk of going missing. They're retired people who have great family support. There is no real reason for their disappearance in circumstances like this. It is a baffling mystery.'

The Wales family attracted a lot of attention from their first media conference. Prudence, Damian and Emma attended as the family representatives. Matthew didn't join them. He said that dealing with the media was 'not his thing'. Prudence told the media that 'we have driven the streets, every track they could have taken [on the way home from Matthew's house] just in case she threw something out of the car, left some sort of evidence. But there is nothing ... We are very fearful for them.'

All three siblings looked worried, weary and wealthy. They didn't look like the sort of family who had ever had any dealings with the police. The story of their missing mother and stepfather interested the journalists. 'Missing Wealthy Couple' was an instant headline. The mystery of the disappearance aroused great public interest. There seemed to be no reason why Margaret and Paul would voluntarily leave their comfortable home, luxurious lifestyle and loving family.

The Wales siblings' reward for enduring the public eye came quickly. By the evening of 10 April, the media net had dragged in one big, silver fish.

Part Four
Finding

To every thing there is a season
and a time to every purpose under the heaven.
A time to be born, and a time to die, a time to plant
and a time to pluck up that which is planted.
A time to kill, and a time to heal,
a time to break down and a time to build up:

The Book of Ecclesiastes

CHAPTER 11

Mercedes

10 April 2002

MARK HESTER IS A CAREFUL MAN WITH A CAREFUL OCCUPATION. As a solicitor, he is paid to look after the small details. When he is at home, he notices things too. It was not surprising then that, on the weekend of 6 and 7 April 2002, Hester noticed a sleek, silver, Mercedes Benz E320 sedan parked in Page Street near the corner of Armstrong Street, Middle Park. The car was not usually parked there when Hester took his dog – or, more accurately, let his dog take him – for their morning walk. He watched the car for five days. It was not moved. The disabled sticker on the right side of the front window bothered him. The car was parked outside an empty house which renovations had reduced to a building site and that seemed an unusual place to park for a disabled person. Surely they would park directly outside the house they wanted to visit? There was no local parking sticker on the car, so Hester knew the driver was a visitor to the area. He noticed other details – the 'Worrells of Toorak' sticker on the rear window of the car, the umbrella on the back window ledge and the large dent in the front near the headlight.

On Wednesday 10 April, Hester watched the ABC television

With her parents-in-law's whereabouts unknown, Maritza tried to maintain some semblance of normality by going to work at Maritza's Imports, her shop in High Street, Armadale.

Once Matthew had been arrested for the murders, his red Nissan Patrol and the trailer he had hired to remove the bodies were taken to the Victorian Forensic Science Centre for examination.

Police investigators found evidence of blood in Matthew's front yard.

By sheer good fortune, the shallow grave was noticed by a park ranger
in bushland near Marysville on 29 April 2002.

Senior-Sergeant Charlie Bezzina and other members of the Homicide squad inspect the bush grave.

A mound of freshly turned over dirt had hidden the bodies, which had been covered by a child's wading pool and secured with bricks and chains.

news at 7 pm. A few minutes into the bulletin, there was a story about a missing wealthy, elderly Armadale couple and their missing, expensive car. He immediately ran outside to the parked Mercedes and took down its registration. A woman from two doors up was there already, doing the same thing. She'd seen the news too. He rang the police.

At 7.40 pm, Constable Pountney and Senior Constable Newton parked their divisional van next to the Mercedes in Page Street. Newton got out a roll of blue and white police crime scene tape and ran it in a square around the intersection. Pountney stopped traffic travelling down Page Street. He opened his notebook and started a crime scene log. No one entered the enclosed part of the intersection without Pountney recording his or her details in the log.

Detectives Fraser, Shiell and Waddell arrived in Middle Park at 8 pm. On the way there, Waddell rang the Victorian Forensic Science Centre (VFSC) and asked for a Crime Scene Unit to meet him in Middle Park. Waddell also rang the Police Transport Branch and organised for a tow truck to come and take the Mercedes back to the Forensic Science Centre once the onsite examination was finished.

Before the Crime Scene Unit arrived in Middle Park, the Homicide detectives conducted a few examinations of their own. With uniformed officers they formed a line search and swept over the intersection, their torches waving in bright yellow circles of light.

Shiell noticed that the Mercedes was parked with the wheels turned to the right. It looked like it had been parked in a hurry. From what the detectives already knew about Margaret Wales-King, she would have been the type to take the trouble to park her $130 000 car neatly. The driver's seat was pulled up close to the steering wheel as if to accommodate a driver of short stature. Even in old age, Margaret was a tall woman.

At 9 pm the Crime Scene Unit arrived. Senior Constable Tracey Starr took two photographs showing an overall view of the Mercedes parked in Page Street. The next day at VFSC, she would take a further ten photographs of the inside of the car. Senior Constable Stuart Bailey of the Crime Scene Unit searched the area around the car and bagged some black tape and an empty Boag's beer bottle back to VFSC. The next day he found nineteen small items worthy of closer inspection in the Mercedes. They included plant buds, leaves, a white pebble, some hairs, two unknown fibres, soil and some blood on the rear seat. Bailey collected DNA swabs from the door handles, the steering wheel, the gearshift, the inside door panels and the door arches. He couldn't lift any fingerprints from the steering wheel. Whoever the driver had been, they'd had enough nous to wear gloves.

Once the Crime Scene Unit had finished their onsite examination, Waddell rang Sally Honan to tell the family that the car had been found. He asked her to find her mother's spare car key and told her to only let two members of the family come to Middle Park. Sally decided that Damian and her brother-in-law, James Connell, should be the ones to go. The sisters were worried that their mother and stepfather's bodies would be found in the boot of the car. None of them were up to seeing their mother in that state.

Whilst James and Damian were heading to Middle Park to see what clues the car held, the Wales sisters went to their other brother's house. Matthew came out to the car – he was full of excuses. He told his sisters that Maritza didn't want him to go out, that she didn't want to be home alone with Domenik. Sally lost her temper with Matthew. She screamed at him that he had to come with them because the police had found the car. Looking back at his front door, Matthew finally agreed and got in the back seat of Emma's car. He started crying and taking great gulps of air as if he were about to faint. His sisters tried to calm him down. The four siblings drove to Emma's house to wait for the call from the police.

Paul King's older brother, Stephen King, was at Emma's. Stephen, a Catholic priest, had flown down from Sydney and was holding a prayer vigil at the house. Everyone in the house joined hands in a circle and prayed in silence. Matthew cried again. The three sisters already felt sure that their mother was dead. However, there was a big difference between feeling and knowing. It was not going to be easy if the police rang and said that Margaret's body had been found stuffed in the boot of her car.

Sally's mobile phone rang. The circle of people stopped praying as she took the call. It was Damian Honan. The car boot was empty. Stephen King started praying again.

Somehow the media heard that the Mercedes had been found. When the reporters and cameramen arrived to look at the wealthy couple's car, Waddell gave an impromptu interview telling them that finding the car was an important part of the puzzle surrounding the couple's disappearance.

The street was filling up with curious neighbours. The media conference had been broadcast all day. A press photographer took photos as the police examined the Mercedes. The *Herald Sun*, one of the two major Melbourne metropolitan newspapers, ran a story the next morning on the discovery of the Mercedes. Its estimated 1.5 million readers learned that the Armadale couple's luxury car had been found and that the police considered the disappearance to be a 'baffling mystery'. Crime Stoppers, the police information service, gave its telephone number for the public to ring in with any information.

The detectives and the uniformed police officers started a doorknock of the nearby houses. In a house in Page Street they found Charles Mouratidis, a night shift driver for a bakery in Clayton. Mouratidis told police that he had noticed the Mercedes when he left for work at 2 am on the morning of Friday 5 April. Mouratidis was sure about the date because it was his first shift back at work after three months off with a bad back. He was equally sure that he hadn't seen the Mercedes parked there before.

Shiell rang the mobile number of the builder working on the house where the car was parked. Steve Larner was helpful. He told Shiell that he had seen the silver Mercedes parked in the same spot on different occasions earlier in the year. Later in the investigation evidence would prove that this was not possible but at the time Larner spoke to Shiell, it was a lead and had to be followed up.

At 10.35 pm, the Mercedes was loaded onto the flat top police tow truck to be taken to the VFSC. The secrets it held, if any, would be revealed over the next few weeks after the forensic scientists had finished their work.

CHAPTER 12

Clues

11 April 2002

ON THE MORNING AFTER THEIR MOTHER'S CAR WAS FOUND, Emma, James Connell and Prudence drove in Emma's black Mercedes to the intersection of Park and Armstrong Streets. Although Prue had had her wedding reception in Middle Park, no one in the family could think of any real link between their mother and the suburb. It was an expensive, upper middle class area like Armadale but south of the city, by the beach, and out of the couple's small comfort zone of the eastern suburbs. The family had so many questions to which they couldn't work out the answers. Why had Margaret and Paul been in Middle Park? Why would Margaret drive there when she hated driving in the dark and didn't like to go too far away from home because of Paul's ill health? What if someone else had driven the car there? Where were they?

The Homicide detectives were trying to answer some of these questions by doorknocking the area. Shiell interviewed Larner, the builder, again. The house next to where the car was parked had a new swimming pool in the backyard. Shiell asked Larner when the concrete had been laid for the pool. It would be a great place to hide two bodies. The builder told Shiell that the pool had been finished long before Margaret and Paul went missing. Some of the other tradesmen working on the site said that they had seen a silver Mercedes parked nearby on several occasions and an older, well-dressed woman get out. As the men were talking, a car just like Margaret and Paul's drove past and parked on the other side of the street. Perhaps an E320 silver Mercedes wasn't that distinctive in Middle Park after all.

Matthew's siblings had decided that they would do what they could to find their mother and stepfather. Family friends offered to help. None of them felt comfortable sleeping in their own warm beds while Margaret and Paul were missing and might be in pain, in danger, or worse.

Emma, James and Prue spent the morning walking around Middle Park looking for any trace of their mother's presence, anything that would help. Like the detectives, they spoke to the builders at the house in Page Street where the car was found. They spoke to people in the street and workers in the nearby shops.

The Armstrong Street shopping area has a supermarket, a few cafes, a wine shop and a bike shop. The wide footpaths are cluttered with tables and chairs and large market umbrellas. By the time the Wales family started their search, the French cafe on the west side of Armstrong Street had already become a media haunt. The owner, who had nothing to do with the disappearance apart from serving coffee to those who were covering it, was interviewed by a newspaper journalist. So was a local bridge teacher who, despite never having met Margaret Wales-King or Paul King, was eager to receive his fifteen minutes of fame for having nothing to say.

The family handed out photocopied posters appealing for information about their mother and stepfather. For months, no telephone pole or shop window in the area was without a black and white photograph of Margaret and Paul, dressed in black tie, smiling.

Reporters hung around Armstrong Street for a week after the car was found. A man who worked in the supermarket told some of them that he had seen a couple matching Margaret and Paul's descriptions on the Tuesday night before the car was found. They were buying dips, he said, and were well dressed in clean clothes. The woman had her hair up and looked like she had been somewhere fancy. The man was confused and had to be helped. For a few days the sighting gave the Wales family some small flicker of hope that Margaret and Paul were still alive. Then, as nothing more came of it and the days turned into weeks, they gave up waiting for good news.

The Homicide Squad detectives arranged for the Real Estate Institute of Victoria to send a letter to its members in the bayside area asking if a couple matching the Wales-Kings' descriptions had contacted any real estate agents to rent or buy property in the last six months. They also doorknocked bed and breakfast places and hotels in the area. One theory that had to be tested was that Margaret and Paul had decided to take a break from their normal lives, without telling their family. Nothing turned up to support that theory.

Each day for the next week, someone from the family went to Middle Park and nearby St Kilda, Albert Park and South Melbourne, and looked. Pacing the streets, Damian, Emma, Prudence and Sally kept hoping they would find something or someone who knew where Margaret and Paul had gone. Strangers called out messages of encouragement. 'I'm sorry to hear about your parents.' 'Good luck, love.' Nobody knew anything. It seemed the Wales family, always so fortunate, had run out of luck.

*

Matthew chose not to join his siblings on their searches, either on the first day after the car was found or any time afterwards. He was busy enough at home.

On 11 April at 3.25 pm, four Homicide detectives, Nazaretian, Van Veenendaal, Fraser and Smith arrived at Matthew's front gate. While they waited for Matthew or Maritza to return home, the detectives took notes describing the house at 1/152 Burke Road, Glen Iris, where the missing couple were last seen alive. A red brick double-storey townhouse with a high rendered brick fence and automated front gate with a secure garage, Matthew's house was only accessible from the inside out. Anyone wanting to get in had to wait for the occupants to unlatch the gate or automated garage door with an internal control. Matthew and Maritza had been renting the house for the last two months, paying $1900 a month for the privilege of doing so.

After ten minutes, Matthew pulled into the drive in his dark red Nissan Patrol. He let the detectives in. Van Veenendaal and Fraser sat with Matthew at his dining table while Smith and Nazaretian took a look around the house. Van Veenendaal, a bulky man with a round face, short dark hair and a thick moustache told Matthew that he had a few questions to ask about his mother and stepfather's disappearance. Matthew nodded his head. 'Yeah, I know that, because I was the last to see them, I understand.'

Van Veenendaal wasted no time beating around the bush. 'Do you know what has happened to your mum and Paul?'

Matthew said, 'No, I don't. They left here on the Thursday after they had dinner and I haven't seen them since.'

'Do you know where they were going after leaving your place?'

'I would say they were going home, they never stay out late.'

'Do you know any reason why they would go to the Middle Park area?'

'No, no I don't.

Van Veenendaal moved on to another topic. Fraser took notes in her daybook.

'What did you have for dinner?'

'Vegetable risotto.'

'Did you have anything to drink with dinner?'

'Yes, wine.'

Van Veenendaal shifted forward in his chair and watched Matthew's face. He knew at this stage that the missing couple had not used their mobile telephone or accessed their bank accounts for eight days. He also knew that at least one member of the Wales family, Damian Wales, had his suspicions about their youngest brother.

'How were your mum and Paul?'

'They were fine, they seemed to be in good spirits. I think Mum had had a little too much to drink before she left.'

'Did they say anything to you about going away somewhere?'
'No.'

'How did you get on with Paul?'

Matthew looked the detective in the eye and said, 'I got on the best with Paul out of all the family, I really liked him.'

Van Veenendaal sat back in his chair and asked Matthew some more innocuous questions about his financial situation. While he did so, Smith and Nazaretian were in Matthew's garage. There was a strange chemical smell in there, the source of which neither police officer could locate. It could have been coming from Matthew's car or the concrete floor. It smelt as if someone had used a very strong cleaning product. Both officers noted it in their daybooks and decided to mention it to Waddell when they returned to the Homicide office.

After leaving Matthew's house, the detectives spread out and knocked on the neighbours' doors. They spoke to the shopkeepers in the milk bar and wine shop across the road. One of the neighbours mentioned that during the weekend his mother and stepfather went missing, she had seen Matthew empty the entire contents of his garage onto the lawn and hose it out with a high-pressure hose. The neighbour hadn't seen Matthew do that sort of thing before and, after seeing the house at number 152 on the news, she thought the police might be interested. They were.

At the same time that Nazaretian, Fraser, Smith and Van Veenendaal were paying Matthew a visit, Waddell and Shiell were back at Mercer Road. Damian Wales was there to meet them. Shiell took Margaret and Paul's computer hard drive, four diaries and address books and a box of floppy discs back to the Homicide Squad for analysis. One of the first things the detectives did was to call any numbers in Margaret's diaries or address books that looked remotely like a Middle Park area number. All the numbers were answered by businesses — a florist, a computer engineer and a chiropractor. The theory that the couple may have driven to Middle Park to spend some time on their own was losing strength with each call.

12 April 2002

At 11.15 am on 12 April, Detectives Nazaretian and Smith went back to Matthew and Maritza's house to follow up the strange smell in the garage. Matthew was home. Nazaretian asked him if he could take his Nissan Patrol away for the day for forensic testing. Matthew agreed. Nazaretian and Smith drove the four-wheel drive to the Victorian Forensic Science Centre in Macleod, a suburb on the edge of bushland in Melbourne's north-east.

Senior Constable Stephen Lake, the crime scene examiner who had searched the house at Mercer Road, was waiting for the car. He spent the afternoon examining it and found nothing of interest save for a *Melways* street directory, with a piece of paper stuck between maps 93 and 94. Van Veenendaal had the car back at Matthew's house by 6 pm that night.

An hour later, Van Veenendaal returned to Burke Road with Detectives Waddell, Smith and Shiell. Forensic officers Deborah Ryan and Howard Hopper were there to meet them. Matthew and Maritza let the officers in. Waddell told Matthew and Maritza that, with their permission, they had come to test the garage floor for the presence of blood. Matthew consented, saying, 'Yes, you have our permission to do whatever you have to do. I understand that we have to be investigated because we were the last people to see Mum and Paul before they disappeared. We will give you as much help as you want.'

Matthew and Maritza watched the testing. Ryan and Hopper taped up the garage so that no light was showing. The Luminol they were about to spray worked better in the dark and so the area had to be sealed. Ryan, a forensic scientist with an honours degree in genetics, sprayed the Luminol, which had been mixed with hydrogen peroxide and water, over the floor of the garage. A compound that produces a chemical reaction with the iron in haemoglobin, Luminol can indicate the presence of blood up to ten years and many attempts at cleaning later. After a few seconds, five small electric blue spots glowed in the pitch black. There was blood in the garage.

At 8.30 pm the police officers made the short trip from Burke Road to Mercer Road. Sally Honan, Damian Wales and James Connell were there to let them in. Ryan repeated the Luminol test on the garage floor, front pathway and entrance foyer of Margaret and Paul's house. This time, no blue spots appeared.

13–29 April 2002

Over the next two weeks, when Margaret Wales-King and her husband were officially missing and unofficially dead, the Homicide detectives' role was to eliminate potential suspects as much as it was to implicate them. The crew working on the Wales-King case met once a day, sometimes twice, in the Homicide Squad offices in St Kilda Road to discuss theories and strategies, information found and material observed. Two whiteboards were used to list ideas and each member of the team was asked to throw in their view for consideration. Before the bodies were found, the whiteboards for Operation Compradore had the names of each adult family member and their spouse on it as a possible suspect. Some of the names were considered to be more possible than others. For most of the detectives working on the case, the focus was always on Margaret's youngest son and his wife because the missing couple were last seen alive at their house. Other members of the Wales family thought he was implicated and Matthew had already exhibited some strange reactions to his mother's disappearance. Despite that focus, the detectives still had to spend hours checking all possible suspects, their financial positions, their relationship with Margaret and Paul and their movements over the weekend they went missing.

During April, every one of Margaret's children and their spouses gave a statement to police. Each of her daughters' ex-husbands was found and interviewed as well. Di Yeldham and Stephen King gave statements about their missing siblings. Yeldham told Shiell that her sister had not been happy about Di's wish to sell their unit in Surfers Paradise and give the proceeds to her children. Rob Lord had left the unit for his daughters to share equally in any income it generated. Di also said that Matthew Wales had told her that he had gone with his mother to put $20 000 from his hairdressing business in her ANZ safety deposit box in the city. Police checked the box and Margaret's other ANZ accounts. Together they held nearly $50 000, not one cent of which had been touched since Margaret's disappearance.

One of Margaret's sons-in-law, Angus Reed, was in Melbourne by himself over the weekend his in-laws went missing. His wife Prudence and their three young boys were in Portsea staying at their beach house for the school holidays. When police questioned Angus he said that he was home the night Margaret had dinner at Matthew and Maritza's. Angus told them that, after working in his investment company's office in the city during the day, he caught a taxi at about 7.30 pm to Romeo's Restaurant in Toorak Village to dine alone. After the meal, Angus walked home. Angus said that he had left a trail of credit card transactions that would support his statement. What Angus Reed didn't have was an alibi for 10 pm onwards, around the time his wife's mother and step-father were last seen alive.

After providing a statement to police on 16 April 2002 in which he said that 'Margaret tried to manipulate her children through the use of money. I used to tolerate her and would say that I was indifferent towards her', it still wasn't clear what Angus John Luxmore Reed had been doing in the late evening on 4 April. He said that he watched television yet couldn't nominate a specific program. Until the gaps were filled, Angus Reed's name would stay on the 'Possible Suspects' side of the whiteboard in the Homicide Squad's office.

The detectives thought that a direct approach would work best with Angus. Like most of his socio-economic bracket, the 36-year-old company director and investor was not used to being re-questioned by highly trained police officers. It didn't take him long to remember that he had been out later that night. On 18 April he made a second statement to Detective Sergeant Van Veenendaal in which he recalled that after work on 4 April he had walked to the Royal City Spa and Sauna in Bourke Street in the city. He had a steam bath and massage before leaving at 9.15 pm. Angus then went back to his office to get some documents and travelled by taxi to Romeo's for dinner. He arrived home at about 11.30 pm. The gaps in his evening were filled and Angus Reed's name could be wiped off the whiteboard.

Throughout the investigation, analyst Helen Nugent continued to filter the Crime Stoppers information and hand out jobs to the Homicide detectives. One report that came to Nugent was about a Mercedes similar to Margaret's being parked around the corner from Mercer Road about the time she and Paul disappeared. The information report said that a young man was sitting in the car 'acting suspiciously'. The detectives did their homework and found the car and the young man. He had been playing truant from a university lecture he couldn't be bothered attending and was sitting in the car for an hour and a half so his mother didn't find out.

The Homicide Squad also relies on information reports from police officers at other stations. They checked all traffic camera information to see if Margaret and Paul's Mercedes had been recorded speeding or going through a red light camera between 4 and 10 April. No records of any traffic violations committed in the Mercedes were found.

During the initial stages of the investigation, some members of the family mentioned to police that Matthew Wales had been involved with some 'shady' Lebanese people through his business as a hairdresser. From March 1997 to December 2000, Matthew had sub-leased part of a hairdressing and hair products shop in Knox Shopping Centre. The owner of the salon, called Hairhouse Warehouse, was Tony Latouff. The homicide detectives went to visit him. They found a sincere, honest businessman who ran a small business with diligence and attention to detail. Latouff considered Matthew a good tenant, always paying his rent on time and treating his staff well. He hadn't seen any disreputable people coming into Matthew's part of the salon. In Latouff's view, Matthew's business was a success and was more so after his marriage to Maritza. Latouff thought that Matthew had a lot of respect for his mother and didn't boast about his family's wealth. In Latouff's opinion, Matthew's dream was to be wealthy in his own right.

As part of the process of eliminating suspects and gathering information, Maritza Wales's sister and brother, Mario and Patricia Pizzaro, were also interviewed. They operate a building and property investment company in the city and did not have any information to shed on the disappearance. Both found their sister to be pretty private about her financial and personal life and did not have the impression that there were any problems at home.

The Wales-Kings were the sort of couple, elderly and wealthy, who relied upon a large number of service providers to keep their lives and home in excellent running order. They employed a cleaner, a bookkeeper, an accountant, a stockbroker, a solicitor and a gardener. They had their Mercedes serviced by Worrells of Toorak and cleaned by a car-cleaning place in High Street, Armadale. They often bought antique furniture from a shop in High Street. Margaret had her hair done every fortnight in a salon in Toorak Road. Paul went one day a week to day care at a local centre. Each and every one of these helpers had to be found and interviewed in case they could shed some light on their customers' disappearance. Despite many hours of interviewing, none of them could.

While the Homicide Squad were busy with their inquiries, the Wales family were making some of their own. They met almost every day to share ideas, theories and their anxiety about what had happened to their mother and stepfather. On 17 April, their father, Brian Wales, flew from his home in England to join them.

During this time Sally, frustrated by not knowing where her mother was, consulted a clairvoyant for guidance. After her session she went to Prue's house to talk about it with Prue, Emma and Matthew. She reported that the clairvoyant had thought that Margaret and Paul had 'taken a substance'. Sally presumed that meant her parents had been poisoned. Emma agreed. Matthew didn't comment and within a few minutes made some excuses and left.

Emma left straight after her brother. She drove down High Street towards her home in Toorak. The traffic was congested and she came to a standstill outside Maritza's Imports. Through the window she could see Matthew in the shop talking to his wife. Her sister-in-law was looking at him with her mouth wide open, in disbelief. He was obviously upset about something, red in the face and waving his arms around. Emma rang Sally on her mobile and told her what she had seen. She was sure her brother was telling Maritza about the clairvoyant's message. Matthew's lack of involvement during the family meetings was becoming increasingly obvious to his brother and sisters. Unlike the others, Matthew didn't have any theories about what had happened to his mother. He contributed little to their conversations, refused to do any media interviews or join in the street searches and, shunning the family dinners, went home in the evenings to Maritza and Domenik.

On 26 April, Brian Wales went to 152 Burke Road to have dinner with his son. Matthew cooked the dinner. During the evening, Brian noticed that neither Matthew nor Maritza mentioned Margaret's disappearance. He asked them if they had actually seen Margaret and Paul drive away and was assured that they had. Matthew drove his father to Sally's house, where he was staying, at 10 pm. Sally, who had felt very uncomfortable about her father going to Matthew's for a meal, was glad to see him.

As the days passed without any concrete information regarding Margaret and Paul's whereabouts, the Wales family turned again to the media for help. Damian, being the eldest son, was nominated as their representative. On 16 April he and Prue gave an interview in which they pleaded with the public to come forward with information that would help them find their mother and stepfather. Damian begged, 'Please, just give us some sort of lead. Please come forward. I don't know why you have hurt our mother or taken her from us. We don't deserve it. We want to know what's happened. It's a very stressful time for us. We're feeling a lot of pain at the moment. We don't know what to think.' He said the grandchildren were feeling the effects of the disappearance. 'We're trying to shield them from it but the older ones are feeling it.' Prue too was desperate for a resolution. 'If we can't have them, we want their bodies.'

Sometimes you have to be careful what you wish for.

CHAPTER 13

Grave

29 April 2002

JON GWILT, A 48-YEAR-OLD RANGER WITH PARKS VICTORIA, had worked in the Yarra State Forest for years. An easygoing man, he preferred the peace of the bush and working with nature to the hassle and rush of the city. On the days following his discovery, Gwilt got a taste of the city life he had left behind.

Gwilt started his shift on Monday 29 April at 8.00 am by driving the Parks Victoria four-wheel drive to the Upper Yarra Dam in the Yarra State Forest. It was a gloriously sunny autumn day and Gwilt was happy to be out of the office. His first job was to unlock the gates that led to the dam catchment area. The forest lies 80 kilometres east of Melbourne's urban sprawl in the Yarra Ranges National Park. A forest of hills densely covered with tall mountain ash trees and gullies of temperate rainforests, the area is an hour and a half's drive from the city's central business district. Bushwalkers, campers and men who hunt and fish are drawn to the park because of its terrain and proximity to Melbourne.

Gwilt had a larger project on his mind that Monday morning. Parks Victoria had decided to close a dirt track, known as Track 3, which ran through the Upper Yarra catchment area. The area was to be closed to protect the water supply for Melbourne contained in the nearby reservoir. Gwilt's job was to arrange the closure by organising a subcontractor with a bobcat digger to place large rocks over the track where it met Woods Point Road. Gwilt drove down Track 3 for about 300 metres. He turned left into a smaller dirt track that was too small to justify having a name, and stopped. Gwilt got out of his car and sprayed two red marks on a rock with a spray gun to show the subcontractor where to start the digging for the closure. He put the spray gun back in the car and walked up the track for about 20 metres. From here, Woods Point Road could not be seen and the few cars that travelled on it could barely be heard.

Gwilt started looking in the bush for large boulders to block the track. He would be able to give the bobcat driver a head start if he knew where to send him. He didn't find any boulders but he did see a mound of dirt, freshly turned over. It looked like a lyre-bird mound. He had seen plenty before. Male lyrebirds built them as a stage for their mating dances. When he got a bit closer, Gwilt changed his mind. The earth was compacted, not something lyre-birds are known to do, and the mound had a couple of large rocks on top of it. Green grass, the sort you'd find in the suburbs, was growing up through the top of the mound.

Gwilt's next thought was that maybe some deer hunters had made a campfire and then buried it after they broke camp. He found some pieces of rope on the ground. Deer hunters often brought hunting dogs with them. Perhaps they had used the rope to tie the dogs up. Gwilt had a funny feeling about the mound. He looked at it more closely. It was oblong, about two metres long and one metre wide. Like a grave. He thought about it and then shook his head. He was being silly. There was nothing to say that someone was buried there. No sign or cross or anything. Gwilt walked back to the car.

He drove to Cambarville and did a couple of maintenance jobs there. As he went about his jobs, the mound kept playing on his mind. He went back to the Parks Victoria office at Woori Yallock with it gnawing at his gut.

Alan Caddy was on a day shift in the office. Over morning coffee, Gwilt told Caddy what he had seen and that he thought it might have been a grave. Caddy offered to go with Gwilt to have another look and sort it out. They got in Caddy's four-wheel drive and arrived back at Track 3 at midday.

Gwilt and Caddy walked up the track to the mound. It *was* the dimensions of a human body. Each tried to convince the other that it was something other than a grave. They started raking off the dirt to see if they could find any rubbish buried, a sign of campers. About ten centimetres into the dirt, Caddy's rake hit something hard and square. He kept raking. Both men reached in and pulled out three concrete besser bricks that had been chained together with a chain and a silver 'D' shackle. They scratched away a bit more dirt. Under the soil there was a blue plastic swimming pool, the sort you blow up for little kids. Gwilt thought they had found a rubbish pile and pulled the pool towards him. Caddy moved the rake through the dirt again. It hit something soft. He brushed away some more soil. There was a cotton bag with a bit of chain looped around one end. Caddy pushed the rake into the bag and pulled it towards him. The cloth tore. That's when the smell came out. It was the smell of something dead. Caddy leant forward. There was a flash of white where the cloth had ripped. It was skin. They had found a body.

Caddy and Gwilt dropped the rake and ran back to the car. Gwilt called the office. Ranger Miles Stewart-Howie took the call. Gwilt told him where they were, what they had found and asked him to call the police. Caddy and Gwilt went back to the mound just to make sure they weren't seeing things. They weren't. They walked back to the car. Stewart-Howie rang again and said the police were on their way. Both men got in the vehicle and drove out onto Woods Point Road to wait for them.

Senior Constable Wayne Phillips, from Warburton police station, south-west of Track 3, was the first police officer to arrive at the grave site. He met Gwilt and Caddy at 1.30 pm at the entrance to Track 3 and wrote down their details. The three men walked back to the mound. Caddy lifted the pool out of the dirt. Phillips saw the cloth, the skin and the chain. He also smelt the smell. Phillips called the Lilydale Crime Investigation Unit. Within minutes, Detective Acting Sergeant Ross Hill and Senior Constable Brigette De Cherico were speeding up the Maroondah Highway towards the grave.

Phillips got some blue and white striped police tape and ran it in a circle around the trees nearest to the grave site. The garish blues of the tape and the pool stood out amongst the soft greens of the bush. For the next twelve hours the dirt mound would become a crime scene abuzz with the Lilydale CIU members, the Homicide Squad, police photographers and forensic scientists working on it, and the surrounding area, like ants at a picnic.

Senior Constable Peter Cox, crime scene examiner, was one of the team working at the site. He removed two cigarette butts and five pieces of rope and twine found near the grave. He also collected the child's pool and the three chained besser bricks used to weigh the body down, the six large rocks placed on top of the mound and some soil samples from the grave. On top of the body, there were some insect eggs and larvae. Cox put them into an exhibit bag to give to a forensic entomologist. They might be useful to determine how long the body had been buried.

Cox had noticed some marks down the walls of the grave. The

tool marks were especially noticeable in the clay layer of soil. There were some flecks of blue-green paint in the grooves of the tool marks. Cox collected a sample of the paint and made a plaster cast of the marks in the dirt.

Just before dinnertime that evening, Detective Senior Sergeant Charlie Bezzina of the Homicide Squad arrived at the grave site and took charge of the crime scene. He looked at the mound of dirt and the wrapped body under the children's pool and decided that it was time to exhume it. The surrounding area could be examined more closely with the body taken out and it would be better to do it before it got too dark. The pool liner was taken off and the body was lifted out. Bezzina bent to look into the grave. There was a second body. It too was wrapped in a doona cover with rope twisted around it and lay the opposite way to the first body. The police photographer leant forward and took photographs of the second body lying in the grave.

Bezzina nodded to the waiting forensic team. They lifted each wrapped corpse into a white body bag and zipped them up. The bags were taken up the track to the government undertaker's hearse.

CHAPTER 14

Autopsies

30 April 2002

IN THE VERY EARLY HOURS OF 30 APRIL 2002, DR MALCOLM Dodd was woken from a deep sleep. As a senior forensic pathologist at the Victorian Institute of Forensic Medicine, Dr Dodd was in the middle of a busy week. His mobile phone was ringing. It was Detective Senior Sergeant Charlie Bezzina. He was up near Cumberland Junction, 100 or so kilometres east of Melbourne, down a dirt road and off a track in the bush. A grave hiding two bodies had been found the day before. The bodies had been carefully exhumed from the grave and the Crime Scene Unit had finished with the area. Bezzina told Dr Dodd that the government undertaker had arrived and was bringing the two bodies to the morgue at the Institute. As the forensic pathologist on call that week, Dr Dodd had to be ready to meet them.

The Victorian Institute of Forensic Medicine, the State Coroner's Court and the Coronial Services Centre are located in Kavanagh Street, South Melbourne. A series of grey and blue cubes, the buildings connect to create one centre devoted to the study of death. Dr Dodd has worked as a forensic pathologist at the Institute since 1995. He is a softly spoken, gentle man whose blue eyes don't give away the horrors he has seen in that time. He and his colleagues conduct about 3500 autopsies a year. In Victoria, a body is sent for an autopsy when the death is unexplained, sudden or suspicious. The bodies that Bezzina sent to Melbourne in the middle of the night qualified for an autopsy on all three counts.

Forensic pathologists work closely with the Homicide Squad on the 100 or so cases a year which are marked as 'suspicious'. Each forensic pathologist is rostered on a homicide roster for one week out of every five. If an autopsy is needed, the Homicide Squad calls the rostered forensic pathologist, day or night, to come to the Institute. In a normal year, each forensic pathologist performs ten to fifteen homicide autopsies.

By the end of April, 2002 was not shaping up to be a normal year for Dr Dodd. The week he received Bezzina's call, Dr Dodd reached a record of six autopsies in a week. He had already performed four autopsies, including one on notorious Melbourne criminal Victor Peirce, and one on a father axed to death by his son.

The forensic pathologist's role in performing an autopsy is to determine the cause of death, to reconstruct the circumstances of death and to provide answers to questions that may not yet have been asked. In looking at a suspicious death, Dr Dodd considers the progression of injuries (which ones occurred when), whether there are any defence wounds indicating that the victim fought back, and whether the victim survived after being injured or died instantly. He also looks for evidence of contact – traces of DNA, fibres or other material left behind by the killer. Ultimately, Dr Dodd gathers information to write a report that can be used as the basis for his evidence in court.

Dr Dodd arrived at the Moore Street entrance to the morgue at about 1.15 am. In the admitting area, the two bodies had already been unloaded from the undertaker's hearse onto stainless steel trolleys. The bodies would stay on the same trolleys during their time at the morgue to prevent any further damage from handling. 'Suspicious' bodies always arrived at the mortuary dressed, unlike 'unsuspicious' bodies, which were stripped. Bezzina had sent the bodies in the same blood-soaked coverings in which they had been found.

Picking up a small tape-recorder, Dr Dodd dictated notes of his initial examination. His first task was to certify that the bodies were dead so that they could be received into the morgue. Bezzina had wanted Dr Dodd to make the certification, rather than calling a local doctor to the burial site, so that the coverings and knots would not be disturbed without a proper record of the way they were found in the grave. By using Dr Dodd to make the declaration of death there would be one forensically experienced doctor handling the bodies. Dr Dodd then had to determine, as far as possible, the bodies' identities prior to their formal autopsies. The bodies before him were wrapped like presents no one would want to open.

Working on the male body first, Dr Dodd cut away the dirty, fine checked doona cover that was trussed together with multi-coloured rope and a heavy metallic chain. He found that the head and neck were covered with several layers of bloodied pea-green cloth. The cloth was kept in place over the head with some elasticised edges gathered together in a knot under the right jaw. Dr Dodd lifted off the green cloth to reveal an elderly man's face. A police photographer took photographs of the coverings, the knots used and the way the heads were unwrapped. He wore a heavy gold metallic chain that was unfastened at the back of his neck. Case number 1244 of 2002 was 'an adult well nourished male of some advanced years'.

The female body, case number 1249 of 2002, was completely enveloped in a green and blue striped doona cover which was bound by metres of multi-twin grey and red flecked rope. The ankles were bound together. Under the striped doona cover, dirty and bloodied plain green material covered the head and neck. Dr Dodd's initial identification was that of a 'well nourished female Caucasian'. Black wire-rimmed glasses were pushed up onto the woman's forehead. The left arm and hand were bent in unnatural angles behind the head. On the left hand, Dr Dodd saw something he didn't usually see on bodies in the morgue – 'Three rings on the fourth digit of the left hand. The largest of the rings comprises a large diamond solitaire. The remaining two rings are smaller, slender, and each contains multiple small diamond insets.'

Once the faces were unwrapped, the bodies were wheeled under a video camera set in the ceiling that took a mortuary identification video. The corpses were then weighed on a large industrial scale built into the floor. A mortuary technician measured the height of each body. They were then wheeled into the morgue fridge to be stored until the formal autopsies could take place.

At a more civilised time during the same day, Dr Dodd dressed in green scrubs and white gumboots and returned to the two bodies in the Homicide Room. A small room separate from the larger, main autopsy room, where up to seven bodies can be examined at once, the Homicide Room is set aside for private post-mortems on suspicious cases. A low-lit viewing room faces the Homicide Room. Divided by a wall of glass, to keep the visceral smells out, the viewing room has high stools from which Homicide police watch the procedure. A microphone set in the glass lets the police talk to the examining doctor while a post-mortem is being conducted.

Detectives Van Veenendaal, Fraser and Waddell had already been in to make a preliminary identification of the bodies at 7.30 am. Detectives Alex Stewart, Wayne Baston and Stuart Cameron were assigned to watch the full post-mortems. Dr Dodd had a forensic technician to assist him, performing the tasks a nurse would if the bodies were alive and this were a normal operation. Dr Dodd performs every autopsy the same way, running slowly through a checklist he keeps in his head. He clears his mind of all emotion before beginning. He cannot afford the luxury of grieving for the victims. The first part of the post-mortem is an external examination of the body.

Dr Dodd removed the coverings from the male body and, speaking into his tape-recorder, described the clothes unwittingly chosen by the victim as his last outfit. Beige trousers, white singlet, long-sleeved blue shirt and a pair of black socks. There were no shoes on his feet. An expensive watch was removed and described – 'Baume and Mercier gold faced quartz movement with a black leather band'. The watch showed the correct time. The man also wore a gold wedding ring.

Dr Dodd methodically examined each part of the body noting its distinguishing marks and features. He found that the body was black and bloated and in a state of advanced decomposition. The changes brought about by the decomposition obscured all but the most obvious signs of external trauma. If the bodies had been dis-covered much later, even the obvious signs might have disappeared. In this case, the injuries not wiped away by the length of time the body was buried were bruising to the face, neck, forearm and leg. Internal examination confirmed that there were three breaks in the nose and middle of face. Patchy haemor-rhages were present under the jaw.

After a thorough external examination, Dr Dodd told the

forensic technician to open the body up. With a small scalpel the technician cut a 'Y' on the front of the chest from the shoulder bone down towards the heart. He then cut a circle around the scalp starting at the back of the head. The organs were taken out in one piece and placed face down in their natural order on a large block to the side of the trolley. The organs and the brain were weighed and examined for signs of illness or trauma.

Dr Dodd took pieces of tissue from the vital organs and placed them in little plastic boxes called cassettes. These would be sent to the forensic laboratory in the same building where forensic scientists would place the boxes into hot wax to make them into thin slides to be examined under the microscope. Samples of blood, urine, bile, liver, eye fluid and gastric content were also sent for testing.

Dr Dodd examined the male body's stomach contents. He noted that the food found was mostly rice and vegetable material that had undergone minimal digestion. The killing had occurred shortly after the victim had eaten a vegetarian meal.

In the comment part of the autopsy report for the male body, Dr Dodd noted that the injuries he could observe on the decomposed body were 'blunt trauma to the face and neck'. These findings suggested that the victim had suffered a hard hit over the face with a blunt object and then 'manual neck compression' or strangling around the throat. Dr Dodd did not think that these injuries alone would have caused death but almost certainly would have rendered the victim unconscious. He thought that there must have been something more that led to death.

Dr Dodd continued: 'the notion of positional asphyxia however cannot be excluded. It is entirely possible that death may have occurred from ... occlusion of the nasal and oral airways during deep unconsciousness.' In Dr Dodd's view, the victim was probably unconscious, and therefore alive, for some time after the assault. He took perhaps an hour or two to slip from unconsciousness to death, lying face down in soil. After more than four hours of cutting and weighing, looking and measuring, Dr Dodd identified the cause of the old man's death as twofold – 'blunt force trauma to the head and evidence of asphyxia'.

Later in the afternoon of 30 April, Dr Dodd started the autopsy on the female body as the same police officers from the Homicide Squad watched through the glass in the viewing room. The pathologist removed the clothes – a singlet, grey slacks, bra, underpants and knee high stockings and the three rings. She was in a better preserved state than the male because of their respective burial positions. The female had been buried underneath the male in a colder, darker spot further away from possible insect or animal attention. He estimated the age of the body as 60 to 70 years. The female's stomach held the same type of vegetable risotto that had been found in the male's and the food was also barely digested. Their last meal had been shared.

Dr Dodd observed scarring on the victim's breasts and a silicone breast implant. She had survived breast cancer at one stage. Scarring on her stomach around the belly button suggested that she'd had a tummy tuck. Samples of blood, hair, muscle and fingernails were taken to the waiting forensic scientists down the corridor. Methodically working through the skeletal system, Dr Dodd noted a fractured nose. There was also a large area of bruising on the neck and the right upper arm. The injuries indicated that the victim might have been strangled.

Dr Dodd conducted further tests on the brain of the female victim. They provided startling results. The brain tissue revealed 'unequivocally that a state of hypoxia has occurred'. The victim had suffered a lack of oxygen prior to her death. Once again, the forensic pathologist found that the fractures and bruises on the body would not have been enough to cause death but would have left the victim unconscious. Dr Dodd felt strongly that the signs of oxygen deprivation indicated that that the victim 'did not die immediately after the alleged assault' but had suffocated later. He concluded that the female, like the male he had examined earlier that morning, had died as a result of 'blunt force trauma to the head and asphyxia'. The detectives left the private autopsy room. They had seen enough to know that the male and female bodies were those of the missing couple. Their ages, clothes and jewellery confirmed what the disfigured faces hinted at. Formal identification was now really only a matter of procedure. It was time to tell the family that their mother and stepfather had been found.

*

Dr Dodd ordered a full toxicology report for the two homicide cases. The toxicologists would look for signs of alcohol and illicit and prescription drugs in the bodies. Once the results came in, Dr Dodd added them to his two post-mortem reports. The tests showed that both victims had consumed normal levels of alcohol, paracetamol and codeine prior to dying. The female had another medication, Atenolol, used for high blood pressure, in her blood. Later, medical records would show that she did not have blood pressure problems and had never been prescribed Atenolol.

Before closing the files on the male and female victims, Dr Dodd had two more experts to consult. Dr Melanie Sian Archer has a pretty name but a very unpretty job. As a consultant forensic entomologist to the Institute of Forensic Medicine, Dr Archer spends her days looking at samples of insects and their larvae found on bodies. She is so passionately interested in her work that she has spent a few thousand dollars installing a microscope at home so she can work at night. During the afternoon when the autopsies were being conducted, Dr Archer went to the Institute and took samples of fly eggs and maggots found on the bodies, their clothes and wrapping. On 2 May she examined the samples and found that 'insect activity on the bodies was characteristic of prolonged burial and the nature of infestation was consistent with burial having occurred soon after death'. She checked with the weather bureau for the temperatures in Melbourne between 4 and 6 April. She found that the temperatures were quite cold and that this meant that blowflies would have been sluggish. Because of this, Dr Archer could not draw any conclusions about events such as the length of time between death and burial.

Dr Pamela Craig, a forensic odontologist or dentist, was contacted and asked to come to the Institute to examine the teeth of the bodies. The decomposition of the bodies meant that they were difficult to formally identify visually. Dr Craig arrived at the Institute early in the morning of 1 May. She conducted a dental examination on the two bodies using normal dental equipment. She took photographs of the intact teeth and the dentures to compare with dental records which the Homicide detectives had collected from Margaret and Paul's dentist. After comparing the teeth of the bodies with the descriptions in the dental records, Dr Craig formally identified case number 1249/02 as Margaret Wales-King and case number 1244/02 as Paul King.

CHAPTER 15

Family

30 April 2002

DETECTIVES STEVE WADDELL AND NARELLE FRASER ARRIVED at Sally Honan's house in Malvern just after breakfast on 30 April. The detectives had come to tell the family that the bodies of a man and a woman, matching the descriptions of Margaret and Paul, had been found in a grave near Marysville and that autopsies would be done that day to confirm their identity.

Waddell had also briefed Detectives Nazaretian and Brundell and asked them to break the news to Matthew and Maritza. At 9.40 am the two detectives paid a visit to the house on Burke Road. Matthew let them into the dining area. The detectives sat down at the same table at which Margaret and Paul had eaten their last meal and told Matthew that there had been a development. Matthew looked down and took a deep breath. His face drained of colour and he fidgeted with his hands under the table. Nazaretian told him that two bodies had been found. He said that while formal identification had not yet occurred, they were probably his mother and stepfather. Nazaretian said that he had wanted to tell him about the discovery before he heard it from the media. Matthew's 'complexion remained pale and he showed no obvious signs of emotion'. When Nazaretian asked him if he had any questions, Matthew said he didn't. Maritza came into the room. Matthew told her what he had just heard. She sat motionless with her head down. Matthew then turned to the detectives and asked them to leave.

As soon as the front door shut behind the detectives, Maritza turned to Matthew. 'Is that where you ...?' She didn't need to finish her question.

'Yes, that's where I put them.'

Maritza leapt up and started pummelling Matthew with her fists. The twenty-seven days of hell she had just endured erupted inside her. She hit her husband in the chest, crying and yelling as she did. Matthew tried to catch her hands and hold her still but she was too upset to be calmed. 'You have to go to the police. You have to go now. I can't stand it anymore.'

'Please don't dob me in, please don't. Just wait, Maritza, please... just wait. I want to spend some more time with you and Dom. Please, Maritza, don't say anything, not yet.'

From the beginning of the investigation, the family had met frequently to discuss possible scenarios that led to their mother and stepfather's deaths and to support each other. Matthew and Maritza rarely joined the family meetings. However, the day the family was told that two bodies had been found all of Margaret's children and their spouses gathered at Sally's house. Throughout the afternoon, the family listened to the local radio news and waited for more information about the discovery. In the early evening, they gathered in the lounge room to watch each of the television stations' news bulletins about the grave site.

Emma Connell looked at her brother and his wife closely as they watched the news segments. She thought that Matthew was oddly emotionless as the newsreaders read details of the discovery of the bodies in the grave. In contrast, Emma saw that her sister-in-law became more and more angry as the segments progressed. When they were over, Maritza, who was standing behind Matthew, had her arms folded in front of her and her head down. Emma told police later that she had the distinct impression that her brother was in trouble with his wife because the bodies had been found.

At 7.55 pm Waddell rang Sally's front door bell for the second time that day. This time, Detective Senior Sergeant Clive Rust was with him. Since his first visit, Waddell had made the three hour round trip to see the burial site for himself. He had also heard the results of Dr Dodd's autopsies. Both officers waited in silence for the door to be answered, heavy with the news they were about to deliver. They had brought news like this to families before and it never got any easier.

The two detectives spent an hour with the family. They confirmed that their mother and stepfather had been found and, picking their words carefully, told them what they could about the state of the bodies and the grave. Waddell described the rings found on Margaret's hand. It was the hardest hour the sisters had spent in their lives.

That news wasn't all that Waddell had to deliver that night. When the meeting with the family was finished, the detective pulled the youngest son aside. He asked him if he would escort the police back to his home. Waddell had a search warrant in his pocket authorising the search of Matthew and Maritza's home. Matthew told Waddell that he agreed to the search and the testing of anything seized during it.

By 10.40 pm Matthew and Maritza's home was crawling with police. As well as Detectives Waddell, Rust, Van Veenendaal, Fraser, Nazaretian, Brundell, Cameron and Stamper, there were four members of the Victorian Forensic Science Centre, Senior Constables Batten, Knox and Hopper, and forensic scientist Stephen Gatowski. All of them were searching the house and garage for anything that would link Matthew Wales to the bodies in the grave.

Hopper took twenty photographs that night. He photographed Matthew's dining area and a suspected bloodstain on the underside of the doormat near the doors that led outside. Officer Gatowski sprayed Luminol over the ground floor of the house. This time there were no blue spots glowing in the dark.

The officers seized a large post-hole shovel, a mattock, three silver 'D' shackles, a ball of green twine and an orange inflatable dinghy that were in Matthew's garage. They also took four rolls of undeveloped film found in the house and the dust bag from the vacuum cleaner in the cupboard under the stairs.

Detective Senior Constable Fraser searched Matthew and Maritza's bedroom. In the middle of the room was a queen-size bed with a curly iron bedhead. On it was a doona in a light blue, white and yellow checked cover. Fraser, having seen the two bodies in the morgue that morning, recognised the doona cover as being similar, in both maker and style, to that used to shroud the male body. She took the cover off the bed and put it in a large exhibit bag to take with her. Before leaving the house, Fraser checked Matthew and Maritza's linen press. There were no other queen-size doona covers in it.

*

Emma wasn't the only Wales sister watching Matthew and his responses to the discovery of the bodies. Sally had become suspicious about Matthew's involvement soon after Margaret and Paul's disappearance. She was very angry with him because he hadn't told her any details of their last dinner together. One day, she and Matthew were at their mother's house together after letting the police in to conduct some forensic testing. Sally was sitting on the bottom stair in the entrance hall and Matthew was perched on an antique chair across from her. She asked him the question that had been burning in her mind.

'Matthew, do you have any idea of what has happened or do you have any theories on their disappearance?'

Matthew didn't look at his eldest sister. He kept his head down on his arms which were cradling his knees. 'I have no idea, Sally.'

Sally knew he was lying.

Prudence was also doing some investigating of her own. Matthew rang her a few days after the bodies had been found and before the funerals were held. Prue told him that the undertaker had warned her that the bodies were very bloated and black. She recalled later that she told Matthew this to 'gauge what his reaction would be'. Prue kept pushing the conversation with her younger brother.

I recall telling Matthew that my life had been destroyed, referring to the fact that my mother had been killed. Matthew's reaction was very strange, questioning me about this. I got the feeling from Matthew's tone that he was surprised by my reaction. I remember thinking (as a result of this call) that Matthew had been the person that had killed my mother and Paul. I got the impression from Matthew that he thought we had all been done a favour by our mother's death.

Despite their fears, the Wales sisters had more traumas to face. They had to say goodbye to their mother and stepfather at a funeral and memorial service without revealing to anyone what they suspected about their little brother.

Part Five
Grieving

The greatest griefs are those we cause ourselves.

Sophocles, *Antigone*

CHAPTER 16

Grief

May 2002

THE FIRST DAYS OF MAY WERE A TIME OF PUBLIC SORROW and mourning for the Wales family. It was also a time of intense speculation, by the media and the public, about the identity of Margaret and Paul's killer.

As soon as it became clear that the bodies found in the shallow grave were those of Margaret and Paul, the media began reporting the police investigation in great detail. Late on Thursday 2 May, the Deputy State Coroner Iain West decided, after hearing a request from Detective Inspector Rix, to put a stop to some of the details being published. He issued a suppression order prohibiting the publication of information about a number of items found at the grave site with the bodies. Rix had sought the Coroner's help after reporters from the *Herald Sun* approached Homicide detectives about what was found in the grave. The police felt that the media were running their own, counterproductive investigation and that it was hampering the efforts of the Homicide Squad to find the killer or killers. Coroner West agreed with them. He made an order prohibiting the *Herald Sun*, or anyone else, from telling the public that a child's swimming pool, three besser bricks and a chain were found in the grave.

Reporters and photographers set up camp outside Matthew and Maritza's house in Burke Road. Some hid in a delivery van and filmed the house. Others filmed using zoom lenses on cameras set up in the upstairs floors of the shops across the road. Each time Matthew or Maritza left the house they were filmed or photographed. Reporters called out questions and thrust microphones in front of them, in the vain hope of getting an exclusive confession. The family was followed when they went grocery shopping or to the park with Domenik. The extensive media coverage of the disappearance and discovery of Margaret and Paul meant that Matthew and Maritza's faces were well known. People stared wherever they went. Whispers followed them. Gossip about the case reached fever pitch. Everyone in middle class Melbourne knew someone who knew someone in the Wales family. Rumours were quickly spread, gaining greater strength with each retelling. Most of the public's speculation about the case cast Matthew as the murderer. Maritza's role was less concrete. Some thought that she was the mastermind behind the killings, others were not so sure. Two theories which gained strong currency in the week after the bodies were found were that Matthew had a drug problem and owed money to underworld figures, or that he had a gambling addiction and was similarly indebted.

On 3 May, Di Yeldham gave an impromptu interview at Matthew and Maritza's front gate. Described as 'courteous but trembling', Di told reporters that the family's grief was being compounded by hurtful speculation about the killers. She said that the rumours surrounding the case were 'unfounded'. Damian Wales was with Di. He told reporters that the discovery of his mother and stepfather's bodies had eased some of the family's pain. The *Herald Sun* quoted Margaret's eldest son as saying 'the first stage is out of the way. We were desperate to find Mum and Paul and there is that great relief that we can actually put them to rest. We just want to get on now and try and find out who's done this. Our minds won't rest until we've actually got a result.'

What Damian Wales didn't tell the reporters was that he and Di had visited Matthew that day to 'put the heat on him a bit to try and get him to tell us more because it was noticeable to us that the police were putting heat on him'. By this time Damian's earlier suspicions that his brother was involved in the murders had hardened into a conviction that he knew who had killed them. Damian thought that perhaps Matthew was being framed for his mother's murder or that the killing was a payback for a debt he owed. During the visit with Di, Damian didn't find out anything new from Matthew. He just confirmed something he had already suspected – that his brother was broke and living beyond his means. Damian left Burke Road thinking that perhaps his younger brother had killed their mother himself to inherit her money.

According to Di's recollection of the meeting, Matthew told her that Maritza's 'old boyfriend' had been hanging around his house. Strangely, he said that, despite this, he wasn't being threatened. Matthew told his visitors that he did not want anything from the family. However, when Di and Damian got up to leave, Matthew asked them if they would stay longer with him. Both refused and left, facing a cluster of reporters and photographers as soon as they opened the front gate. Reporters rang Matthew's intercom to see if he would speak to them after his aunt and brother's visit. Matthew said, through the intercom speaker, that he was 'not too good at the moment. I'm too emotional about this whole situation to speak'.

Matthew had plenty of reasons to feel emotional. The Homicide Squad detectives were putting the heat on him. His telephone calls were being taped by listening devices and his home was under constant police surveillance. Before the discovery of the bodies, all roads had led to Matthew. After they were found, the roads quickly turned into a freeway. A freeway carrying some pretty heavy traffic.

In the week of the funeral and memorial services, a number of pieces of evidence fell into place. The items found during the search of 1/152 Burke Road on 30 April provided the Homicide detectives with a plethora of clues linking Matthew to the murders. The green twine found in Matthew's garage matched the twine at the grave. The 'D' shackles seized were identical to the one used to connect the chain around the male body. The blood spots in Matthew's garage were analysed and found to be human blood.

There is a saying within the police force that the three motives for murder are love, hate and greed. With the last of these in mind, Homicide detectives asked Matthew and Maritza for copies of their bank account and credit card statements. On 6 May they went with Maritza to her shop to gather some more information about her and Matthew's financial position. Members of his family had been pulling the detectives aside to mention that their youngest brother and his wife were living way beyond their means. The investigating police knew that living a champagne life on a beer budget could lead to difficulties and frustration, especially when the other members of the family were wealthy.

Matthew and Maritza's bank account statements and the books for Maritza's Imports were analysed by Gerard Curtain, a senior investigator with the Major Fraud Group of the Victoria Police, who is also a chartered accountant. He found that, in the year before Margaret and Paul's disappearance, Matthew and Maritza had spent about $900 more than they earnt. Curtain found that while their nine-month-old business was in debt to the tune of about $52 000, he could not draw any conclusions about its long-term prospects.

Detective Andrew Stamper was given the task of reading through more than a year's worth of credit card statements. On 3 May, Stamper came across an entry in Matthew Wales's Visa statement that showed he had spent $103.54 at Toys-R-Us in Melbourne Central shopping centre on 11 January 2002. Stamper got on the phone to Kevin Rees, the investigations officer for the store, to find out what Matthew had bought that day. Rees went through the books and found that Matthew had gone through register 9 and bought some lollies, three plastic balls, an air pump and one Cloverleaf Swim Centre Pool. The pool was the same brand as the child's pool used to line Margaret and Paul's grave. When the police had searched Matthew and Maritza's house and garage three days earlier, the pool was not there.

While Stamper was ringing Rees, another member of the Homicide crew, Detective Senior Constable Stuart Cameron, was in West Melbourne taking a statement from Scott Turley. Turley had worked for the previous two years as a console operator at the Mobil service station on the corner of Waverley and Burke Roads, East Malvern. The station is a stone's throw from Matthew and Maritza's house at 1/152 Burke Road and provides hire trailers as well as the usual services. Turley recalled that he started work at 6 am on 5 April and that by 7.20 am he had hired out two trailers. The second customer used eftpos to hire a small, six foot by four foot, blue Tandec box trailer and buy one 'D' shackle. In order to hire a trailer the customer must provide a driver's licence and fill in personal details on a hire form. The service station keeps one copy of the form and the other is given to the hirer. Turley's second customer was Matthew R. Wales of 6 Horace Street, Malvern who was born on 18 February 1968. The trailer was returned on Monday 8 April at 3 pm. After taking the statement, Cameron made arrangements to have the trailer taken to VFSC for forensic testing.

Cameron wasn't finished his day's work yet. He had been speaking to Julie Hayes, the owner of Tait Timber and Hardware in Glen Iris. He had asked her to look through her business's credit card and cash sales dockets for any sales of 'D' shackles, galvanised chain, sash cord, silver rope, green baling twine and blue crowbars during 4, 5 or 6 April 2002. On 3 May, Hayes went through the dockets and called Cameron. She had found a transaction that went through at 8.45 am on 5 April. A customer had used cash to buy five 'D' shackles, five metres of sash cord and six metres of galvanised chain. Cameron drove to Tait's to collect a copy of the docket and speak to the cashier who had made the sale. Teresa McGlashan was working at Tait's on the morning of 5 April. She was shown the docket Hayes had found. It had her initials on it. She told Cameron that she couldn't remember the customer but she was certain it was a man. She had never sold a woman six metres of chain.

The next day, 4 May, Cameron was back on the hardware trail. He spoke to Geoffrey Powell, the owner of Dean's Hardware in Glen Iris. Matthew's Visa card statements showed that he had made a $74.45 purchase there on 6 April 2002. Cameron wanted to know what Matthew had bought. Powell went back through the shop records and found the receipt. Matthew had been shopping for a mattock, a tool which has a wooden handle like an axe and two blades, a wide one for digging and another narrower one for chipping or cutting. He had also bought industrial strength cement cleaner called Liquid Magnet. Cameron took a copy of the receipts.

The detective had one more inquiry to make. Matthew's Visa card statement referred to a purchase from Fulton's Garden Supplies in East Malvern on 6 April. Cameron spoke to Glen Bigger, a sales assistant with Fulton's. He remembered serving a customer who wanted some Surecrop compost delivered on Monday 8 April. The delivery address was 1/152 Burke Road, Glen Iris. Cameron added that receipt to his collection.

On 4 May Jamie Tonkin, deer hunter, was at a birthday party for his favourite uncle. Uncle Graham had introduced Tonkin to deer hunting and a lot of his hunting friends were at the party. Tonkin pricked up his ears when some of the blokes started talking about the bodies that had been found off Woods Point Road. The hunters had heard that the bodies were a rich couple from downtown. Tonkin rang Lamont the next day. They worked out that they had seen the Nissan on the weekend the bodies were meant to have been buried there. On 6 May, Tonkin rang the Warburton police station and told the constable who answered the phone about the car and trailer he had seen about a month earlier up near where the bodies were found.

A few minutes after his call, Tonkin got a call from Detective Narelle Fraser from the Homicide Squad. She asked Tonkin a few questions about what he had seen and where he had seen it. Pretty quickly, Fraser realised Tonkin had something useful to say. She told him to stay where he was and that she would be up to see him straight away.

A few hours later, Tonkin had Fraser and Van Veenendaal on his doorstep. They asked him again what he had seen. Van Veenendaal asked Tonkin if he could show them the place where he had seen the Nissan pull out. Tonkin didn't have a job and his wife was busy with their new daughter, so he agreed to go with the detectives then and there.

Tonkin sat in the back of the detectives' unmarked police car and told them where to go. Once they got to Woods Point Road, Tonkin made Fraser drive along it until they reached Track 25. Once they got there, Tonkin knew they had come too far and made her turn back and pass another unmade road known as Track 3. At the Big River end of Woods Point Road, Track 3 comes into the sealed road at right angles. The three of them got out of the car and started walking down the track. Tonkin stopped at the place where he had seen the Nissan and told the detectives he was '100 per cent confident' that was the spot. He was standing metres from where Margaret Wales-King and her husband had been buried.

*

Each member of Margaret's family was asked to provide a DNA sample to compare it with DNA discovered on items found with the bodies. On the afternoon of Sunday 5 May, the family gathered at Sally's house. Steve Waddell and Narelle Fraser had been to take everyone's DNA sample using an oral swab. Each of Margaret's children, except Matthew, had rolled the swab around the inside of their cheeks and given it to Fraser who put them into small exhibit bags. Matthew told Waddell that he had been advised by his lawyer not to provide a sample. He said to the detective, 'Don't worry, one day you'll get it.'

Later, Emma asked Matthew why he had refused to give a sample. Matthew said, 'I'm protecting my family.'

Emma was incredulous. 'We are your family!'

'No, my direct family – Maritza and Domenik, I have to protect them.'

'From what?' Emma glared at her brother. 'We are looking for the murderers who killed our mother –'

Matthew leapt out of his seat and lunged towards Emma, roaring, 'Don't you start.' Brian Wales and Di Yeldham grabbed him and pulled him down. Brian screamed at his daughter, 'Just go outside, Emma, give it a rest.' She left the room and went into the garden.

Brian Wales was shocked by his son's outburst. He recalled later that seeing Matthew's anger made him think that he was quite capable of killing Margaret and Paul.

After a while, Matthew followed Emma outside. Sally, Damian and Prue were with her. 'I know you guys don't understand my decision, but my solicitor has said not to give DNA as the cops could frame us. You don't understand, I have to protect my son . . .' Matthew burst into tears. Sally, Damian and Prue put their arms around him. Sally pulled her brother onto her shoulder. 'We love you, Matt, we just need to know the truth.' Emma turned away and went inside, slamming the door behind her.

*

As children of a murdered woman, every aspect of the Wales siblings' grieving was scrutinised and reported. Soon after the identification of Margaret and Paul's bodies, death notices started appearing in the Melbourne metropolitan newspapers. The notices were long, floral and expensive. Each sibling and many of the grandchildren placed a separate notice. Like the others, Matthew, Maritza and Domenik wrote directly to Margaret: 'Sleep peacefully love is always near and those special moments never disappear. Adored and forever in my heart I will miss you forever. Loved and respected by those around you and a pillar of strength that will always see over all that were close. Thank you.

Love always Matthew, Maritza and Domenik.' Matthew's tribute to Paul was more succinct and less poetic: 'The loving memories of my second father and loving husband to Margaret. May they both rest in peace. Matthew, Maritza and Domenik.'

In many Melbourne households, amateur sleuths pawed over the notices for clues to the murderer's identity. Satisfyingly, both Prue and Emma referred to the fact that the murderer of their mother had not been caught. Emma appealed to her mother for help: 'So for now we go on wondering what the real truth might be, if you ever want us to know it will you please set it free?'

Prue wrote to her mother that 'My promise to you is justice.'

In death as in life, Paul King was barely noticed. Neither Sally nor Damian, Margaret Wales-King's eldest children, lodged a death notice for Paul or mentioned him in their mother's tribute. Sally told police that she had only tolerated Paul. Damian told them that he still felt a lingering resentment about Paul's responsibility for the break-up of his parents' marriage and his father's subsequent depression. Among all the notices, there was a single description of Paul. Prue wrote that he was 'a gentle soul'. She was the only stepchild to thank him for the years of love and care he gave to her mother.

The tributes were not immune from media commentary. The *Herald Sun* and the *Australian* newspapers ran articles summarising the death notices. The *Herald Sun* article referred to the death notices located further on in the same paper.

On Tuesday 7 May the family was told that the bodies were ready for viewing. A month after Margaret and Paul had been reported missing, the formal grieving process could begin. Even though the funeral director had warned the family that the bodies were black and bloated, they wanted to see their mother and stepfather one last time.

The two coffins were prepared for a rosary service in Mulqueen's private chapel in Burwood. Relatives were invited to pray for the souls of Margaret and Paul before the family mass the next day.

Prior to the rosary starting, the Wales sisters, their spouses and Damian gathered in the foyer of the chapel. Other members of the extended Wales, Lord and King families joined them. Matthew and Maritza were not in the foyer by the time the Catholic priest arrived to begin the rosary. The sisters were worried that their youngest brother and his wife wouldn't arrive in time for the service. The double doors to the chapel were opened and the relatives filed in. Margaret and Paul's coffins were at the front of the chapel, under the altar. It was the first time Margaret's children had been near her body since her death. Emma remembers feeling light-headed at the thought of seeing her mother and stepfather again. Sally, Prudence, Emma and Damian walked straight to their mother's coffin. Huddled over, they touched her coffin and cried. They whispered the things they had been cheated of saying to her while she was alive.

Matthew and Maritza were already seated in the second row from the front. They had been there while the rest of the family gathered in the foyer. Emma noticed that the couple were the only people in the chapel not crying, not swept up in the emotion of being confronted by the reality of Margaret and Paul's death. After a while, Matthew stood up and approached his mother's coffin. He held on to its sides as if it were a life raft and started sobbing. 'Mamma, Mamma.' Matthew's cries filled the small chapel. The quiet sniffles and tears of the other mourners were drowned by his voice.

Damian was standing next to Paul's coffin. For the last twenty-five years he had thought of Paul as his mother's shadow, as an extension of his mother. Now, even in death, Paul King had followed Margaret. Damian wanted to say goodbye to the man who had been so loyal to his mother. When his brother started sobbing, Damian looked at him with disgust. He was convinced that Matthew had something to do with the murder of his mother and stepfather and to see him wailing on this night made him furious. Damian's anger was not unnoticed. His wife, Liz, and Emma came to his side and led him back to his seat. Emma whispered in her brother's ear, 'We're here for Mum and Paul and not for him.'

Emma recalled later that during the service she noticed Maritza cleaning her boots – 'she seemed uninterested and I was very offended by this'. After the rosary, the relatives filled the foyer. Prudence noticed that Matthew and Maritza didn't join them. She said that Maritza walked out of the funeral parlour with her head down and didn't say anything to anyone.

Emma was hosting a dinner for mourners at her home in Toorak. A great-aunt, Olga Lord, was having people back to her house as well. Matthew and Maritza didn't go to either function – they went home to Glen Iris.

The next day, Wednesday 8 May, a private funeral service for the families was held at St Peter's Church in Toorak Road, Toorak. The church was as close to a family church as the Wales could get. Margaret and her daughters' school, Loreto Mandeville Hall, used St Peter's as its church and the family had occasionally attended services there as school students and adults. When the foundation stone of the church was laid in 1933, the then Archbishop of Melbourne, Dr Daniel Mannix, noted that: 'Until recently Catholics did not make much impression on Toorak, but now Catholic institutions in Toorak include Loreto Mandeville Hall and St Kevin's College.'

Forty members of the families said goodbye to Margaret and Paul in a one-hour service inside the early Gothic church's stone walls. Two plain-clothes detectives sat with the families. Damian Wales delivered the eulogy on behalf of both families. His voice broke as he spoke of his love for his mother and the families' grief at the way she and their stepfather had died.

After the service the Wales siblings, their spouses and some of their children came out of the church's closed dark red doors into the flash of cameras and the probing microphones of the media. Despite the families' decision to keep the location of the funeral service a secret, television crews and press photographers had gathered in the church's car park. The television cameras started rolling when the doors opened and the reporters rushed forward, hoping to get a glimpse of the Wales children, and in particular Matthew, in mourning.

The siblings each sprinkled holy water on the two flower-covered coffins and then followed them to the waiting hearses. The reporters watched their every move and emotion and were especially interested in Matthew's reactions. That morning the *Herald Sun* had reported that the Homicide Squad had seized a trailer 'allegedly' hired by Matthew from a service station near his house, hours after Margaret and Paul were last seen alive. The article also reported that police were following up reports from neighbours that Matthew was seen hosing out his garage soon after the disappearance. In an article that didn't mention Matthew, *The Age* reported that police had seized a trailer 'they believe may have been used to transport the bodies of Armadale couple Margaret Wales-King and Paul King hours after they were murdered'.

The next morning *The Australian*, a respected national paper, carried the headline on page one – 'Family mourns as suspicions swirl'. The article singled out Matthew's reactions at the family funeral and referred to his alleged trailer hire. The *Herald Sun* devoted its cover to the family funeral service. In a report titled 'Goodbye – son's tears for murdered mother' the paper described Matthew breaking down in tears at the funeral and wiping tears from both his cheeks as he hugged Damian on the steps of the church before the service. More than one reporter noted that Matthew was the last to sprinkle holy water on the coffins and that, after he had done so, he went and sat with Maritza in a black limousine. Outside the church, the rest of his family hugged and comforted each other.

The hearses turned out of the church into Toorak Road and began a procession to the Necropolis crematorium in Springvale Cemetery. At the crematorium, four cremators were burning at nine hundred degrees Celsius. On arrival, Margaret and Paul's coffins were given reference numbers so that they would not be confused with the other twenty-eight coffins received for cremation that day. Two cremators were cleared and the two coffins were placed inside. The flames rose and covered the coffins. Ninety minutes later, they stopped. Two piles of ashes were raked into fawn, sealed, weatherproof, rectangular boxes. A funeral director from Mulqueen's Undertakers collected the boxes. At the funeral parlour, he put the regulation issue boxes into ornate wooden boxes in preparation for the memorial service the next day.

The Wales and King families went back to Emma's house in Toorak for lunch. Matthew and Maritza did not join them.

On Thursday 9 May, it became clear that Margaret Wales-King was one of those Catholics who had made an impression in Toorak – her memorial service was attended by more than 700 mourners and scores of reporters. Despite the grey skies and threat of rain, the media again filled the driveway of the church.

Television stations' vans and mourners' cars clogged Toorak Road. The photographers snapped photographs of the Wales siblings arriving in their black chauffeur-driven cars. The reporters noticed that Matthew and Maritza were the last to arrive. In spite of their grief, the family put on a brave face and were well dressed and groomed. The sisters had been at the hairdresser's at 7.30 am to get their hair done for the occasion.

The traffic for the memorial was so busy that St Peter's Early Learning Centre for pre-school children, behind the church, had to close its doors for the day.

Sally had reserved the front rows of pews in the church for the Wales family. Once she sat down, she noticed that Matthew and Maritza had chosen seats a few rows back from the immediate family. Nor could she see any of Maritza's family at the service. Sally decided it would not be politic to make a fuss and get Matthew and Maritza to move to sit with the rest of the family in front of a church filled with people. She left them where they were.

Hundreds of darkly dressed mourners signed condolence books in the foyer of the church and then squeezed onto the slim wooden pews to listen to the service conducted by the parish priest, Monsignor Gerald Cudmore and Paul King's brother, Father Stephen King. Father King had returned to Melbourne from his home in a Marist community in Sydney's northern suburbs to bury his younger brother. Margaret's sister, Di Yeldham, and her three children, Ali, Rebecca and Joshua, had also made the trip from Sydney to farewell Margaret. Many of Melbourne's upper class sat in St Peter's that Thursday morning. One reporter described them as a 'smart lot, the men in suits, the women mostly blonde and nearly all in black, except for a couple of Toorak lasses who turned up still in their gym gear'. In amongst the congregation sat Detectives Van Veenendaal and Rust. They were there as a sign of respect to the victims and not, as indicated in the media, to watch the mourners.

Damian Wales delivered his second eulogy in as many days. This time, he spoke softly but his voice could not hide his anger about the way his mother had died. He described her as a 'beautiful and loving woman' who 'showered us with affection'.

Margaret, he said, would have wanted those gathered 'to turn the other cheek' to the way her and Paul's lives had ended. Damian wasn't prepared to do that. He made a vow to the hundreds of people sitting before him that 'justice will be done'.

Di Yeldham delivered a eulogy about her sister. She told the congregation that Margaret was 'an inspirational woman' and 'a leader'.

Emma took her place at the podium and read, in a quavering voice, a passage from the Book of Ecclesiastes:

To every thing there is a season and a time to every
purpose under the heaven:
A time to be born, and a time to die, a time to plant
and a time to pluck up that which is planted.
A time to kill, and a time to heal, a time to break down
and a time to build up.

Sobbing, Prudence and Sally read two more Bible passages. Matthew read a short prayer of intercession.

After an hour the service was over. The family moved to the front of the church and placed small white candles in front of the ornate wooden boxes holding Margaret and Paul's ashes. As they lit them, the tune of 'Time to Say Goodbye' filled the church. Many of the mourners started crying. The boxes were carried out of the church and into the hearses.

Damian Wales stood at the door of the church and shook hands with mourners and thanked them for coming to the memorial. Matthew and Maritza went straight to a black limousine.

In her fourth statement to police a month after the memorial service, Emma Connell was scathing about her younger brother and sister-in-law's behaviour throughout the services:

> To my knowledge, Matthew had no input into the funeral arrangements at all whereas everybody else did. Matthew didn't even ask anybody what was planned or what was happening after the funeral. We had to inform him that cars for the memorial service would collect him and the wake after the funeral would be at [her house in] Orrong Road. I did notice that he sprinkled holy water over the caskets when the family were invited to do so – this is one of the few times I saw Matthew actually do anything. I didn't see Maritza partake – I think she had already gone to the car. Maritza never spoke to me this day – in fact I actually approached her at the start of the funeral and gave her a peck on the cheek and she didn't even respond. I found this incredible. I actually said to her 'How are you going?' and she never responded. It was like kissing a marble statue.

*

Margaret's solicitor for the last twenty-four years of her life, Anthony Patrick Joyce, was not at her memorial service on 9 May. Despite having been to her children's weddings and having dinners with Margaret and Paul over the years, he had other, more pressing things to do that day. Joyce had filed an application on behalf of the estate of Margaret Mary Wales-King in the Probate

Jurisdiction of the Supreme Court of Victoria on 7 May. The application was heard as Margaret's ashes were being escorted from St Peter's Church. Joyce asked the Supreme Court to appoint him as a temporary administrator of his client's large estate until a full grant of probate could be made. In an affidavit supporting his application, Joyce listed Margaret's assets as including the townhouse at 40 Mercer Road, Armadale (worth an estimated $1.5 million); the contents of the home including antiques (worth an estimated $800 000); jewellery worth more than $130 000; the silver Mercedes E320; bank accounts holding around $50 000; a share portfolio worth over $3 million and a joint share holding with Paul King worth $88 000. Joyce also filed a copy of Margaret Wales-King's last will, dated 17 August 1990, which provided that the estate be divided equally among her five children with the stipulation that each child receive their share as they turned forty. Joyce told Detective Van Veenendaal that he would be surprised if any of Margaret's children knew about the contents of her will as his client was extremely private about her financial affairs.

An application such as Joyce's, for letters of administration, known as *ad colligendum, bona*, is a rare step. However, neither Margaret's death nor her wealth were ordinary and Joyce made the application to secure the estate until the police investigation was finished. Under the will, four executors and trustees of the estate were nominated – Paul King, Tony Joyce, Matthew and Damian Wales. Joyce was asking the court to appoint him as a temporary administrator, therefore overriding the terms of Margaret's will, until the division of her estate could be considered properly. Both Matthew and Damian sent paperwork to the court agreeing to Joyce's proposal. Joyce told the Supreme Court that his request to take care of the estate was partially based upon confidential information he had received from the Homicide Squad. Justice Ashley agreed with the course of action Joyce proposed. The solicitor became the temporary administrator of Margaret's estate. Neither Matthew nor Damian, nor their sisters, were able to access it.

The night of the memorial service, Sally Honan rang her youngest brother. She asked him why he had not spoken to anyone at the service and had left immediately. Matthew said, 'I feel empty, I didn't feel like socialising. I just want to be alone with Domenik. I didn't say anything to anyone. I haven't even spoken to Maritza properly yet. Look, Sally, when I am ready I will talk to you. I just need some more time.'

'Matt, do you want to tell me anything?' Matthew was silent. Sally could hear him breathing. 'Do you?'

' Sal, I just want to be alone.'

'Well, you know, I am your greatest friend at the moment.'

'I – I just want to be alone.'

'That night – I would have been the person to call.'

'I just want to be alone.'

'I know, I know where you were at.'

'No – no you don't.'

'Yes, I do.'

'Sal, nobody knows where I am at.' Matthew started crying.

'Matt, whatever happened, we will work through it together, okay?'

'Yeah – I – I just want to be alone for the time being. I'll speak to you later.'

'Promise.'

'Yeah – I promise.'

'Matt, don't make any big decisions without talking to me first – okay?'

'Okay, Sal.' Matthew hung up. The Homicide Squad had placed a listening device on his home phone. It recorded the whole conversation.

The day after the public memorial service, Friday 10 May, the papers printed a photograph of Maritza dabbing at her eyes with a handkerchief and Matthew glaring at the media, his dark eyes angry under his shaved head. By then, his brother and sisters, along with most of Melbourne, believed that Matthew Wales had killed their mother.

On Friday morning, Damian, Emma and Prue braved the media gathered around 1/152 Burke Road to visit Matthew. After the visit, Damian told reporters that the siblings had spent the time having a 'family chat' and mourning session. In fact, Matthew had told his visitors that he could not discuss anything with them because his lawyer had advised him not to.

Finally, on Saturday 11 May, the family could quietly bury their mother and stepfather's ashes at Sorrento. The beach village held many memories for them as they had spent endless summers and school holidays there as children in the family beach house. In later years, both Prudence and Sally had their own beach houses in the area and Margaret and Paul's property at Red Hill, on the Mornington Peninsula, was only a twenty-minute drive up and over the hill from the beach.

The Wales family, Di Yeldham and Brian Wales took the ornate wooden boxes to Sorrento Cemetery to bury the ashes. Emma told reporters that the burial was 'a final word in a chapter of their lives, and they've been laid to rest now where they deserved to be'.

Matthew and Maritza were not at Sorrento. They were wanted elsewhere.

CHAPTER 17

Counsel

May 2002

PHILLIP DUNN QC HAS CHAMBERS AT THE TOP OF A BUILDING in Lonsdale Street, a short walk from the Supreme Court. His room on the eleventh floor is genteel and discreetly affluent, much like its occupant. A haven of red leather and Aboriginal art, Phil Dunn's room has heard many sad stories and secrets. A criminal barrister for more than three decades, Dunn has a jovial and generous manner that hides the seriousness of his practice. When asked how he is, Dunn always replies in the uber positive – 'fabulous, fantastic, terrific'. Surprisingly for a man whose vocation is to speak for others, and unlike many of his peers, Dunn is also a good listener. Over recent years Dunn has listened to Gary Ablett, Frank de Stefano, Carmen Lawrence, John Elliot and Alan Bond.

In late April and early May 2002, Phil Dunn received two visitors seeking the benefit of his silver tongue and golden mind. Di Yeldham was the second visitor to the eleventh floor eyrie. She had met Dunn socially through the South Yarra set and thought he was the right sort of counsel to defend her nephew, Matthew Wales. Dunn remembered Di Yeldham as a friend of his neighbour's and as a woman often reported in the social pages of one of

Melbourne's daily newspapers, *The Age*. The day she visited Dunn, Di had more than high society on her mind; she was trying to defend the family honour. Di told Dunn that she kept thinking about what Margaret would have wanted her to do. Di knew that she wanted to get the best barrister she could for Matthew.

What Di didn't know was that Dunn had moved from the South Yarra hill to sunny St Kilda, where he was enjoying a new lease on life living behind a Brazilian wax parlour, and that he already had a brief in the Wales-King case. Maritza Wales had paid him a visit.

Di left Dunn's chambers and knocked on Robert Richter QC's door, three doors down the corridor. Richter, a fiery red-headed character, was Dunn's contemporary and equal. For years the two have shared work, with the 'A' list of white-collar criminals, and play, with their families going on regular overseas trips. Richter recalls the visit from Di with great clarity. A barrister has only three things to sell to a prospective client – integrity, independence and reputation. Di Yeldham wanted Richter to defend Matthew Wales in a manner that would compromise all three. As Richter colourfully puts it – 'she wanted to nobble me'.

Di wanted the best for Matthew but on the family's terms. She asked Richter to be her nephew's counsel on a conditional basis. The condition was that he not denigrate the family or make any adverse remarks about them throughout the plea. Richter, like most barristers who take their profession seriously, refused to accept a brief that would compromise his independence. He told Aunty Di to take a hike.

A week or so before Di Yeldham's visit, Phil Dunn had accepted a brief to act for Maritza Elizabeth Wales. He recalls jumping at the chance to be her counsel. In his long career he had acted in nearly a hundred murder cases but never for a wife in

Maritza's position. He first met Maritza one weekend in late April when she and Paul Galbally, her solicitor, came to his house.

Unlike Dunn, Paul Galbally comes from a long line of lawyers. Criminal law stories ran through his childhood like fairytales. Galbally has dark brown hair with a splash of white at the front, blue eyes and a kind and gentle manner. He has worked in criminal law for thirteen years without any of its harshness affecting his soft nature. Maritza was referred to Galbally by Matthew's solicitor, Steve Pica. Pica hadn't thought it appropriate to act for both of them. When Galbally first met his new client, her calmness and courage impressed him. Although she was visibly upset by the situation in which she found herself, the solicitor thought she had an enormous amount of dignity that would see her through the trials ahead.

In their initial meeting, Galbally and Dunn explained to Maritza that they were independent and could not be influenced by anyone. They told her that they took instructions only from her and that the Wales family, including Matthew, had nothing to do with the information she would give them. Maritza's immediate problem was the request from the police for a DNA sample. She didn't know what she should do. Matthew was telling her she shouldn't do it. Dunn and Galbally told her to provide a sample.

Throughout the meeting, Maritza kept looking out the window. Matthew was outside, pacing up and down the street. Maritza left after a few minutes. Both lawyers thought she had more to tell them.

A few days after the weekend meeting, Maritza took the lift to the eleventh floor. She was meant to be at her shop, Maritza's Imports, but she had closed it early to make the trip into the city. Matthew was at home with Domenik and didn't know she was there. Dunn saw her sitting on the red leather couch in the waiting area when he got back from court. When she saw him, Maritza jumped up and told him that she had to go, that she was late, and rushed to the lift. She did the same thing again a few days later.

The third time Maritza took the lift up to the eleventh floor, Dunn made her stay. He called Paul Galbally and told him to come over immediately. Dunn put the kettle on and made Maritza a cup of tea. When Paul Galbally arrived, the two men arranged themselves in the antique chairs and looked at Maritza.

In his gentlest voice, Dunn said to her, 'I think there is something we need to talk about.'

Maritza trembled and hugged her arms around herself. Tears rolled down her cheeks. She started whispering. 'I don't know what to do. Matt is saying he will go to the police and sort it out. I don't know, I've been asking him to for weeks.'

Dunn and Galbally let her talk. She told of the weeks of anguish she had suffered, how she hadn't been able to tell anyone what had happened and that she was worried about what was going to happen with Domenik. After a while, as it got darker, Maritza began to worry about getting home on time. She told the lawyers that she would leave it to them to decide what to do and went home.

That night Galbally and Dunn spent many hours working out a strategy for their client. Dunn knew that they had to contact the Homicide Squad on her behalf. He also knew that in dealing with police prior to a confession it was vital for the police to believe his client. One way to convince the police that Maritza was telling the truth was to give them something they didn't already know and that could only be known by someone who knew the true events of 4 April. Dunn and Galbally worked out their approach on a whiteboard in Dunn's room. They drew up alternative paths and what would happen if they took them, for better or worse. Finally, they decided on an approach. Dunn rang the Homicide Squad. The receptionist answered the phone and told him that all the detectives were busy and he could leave a message. Dunn, feeling a little deflated, left a message and waited for a detective to call him back.

Two days later, Dunn and Galbally met with Inspector Brian Rix and six of the detectives working on the Wales-King case. The meeting was a stony affair. The Queen's Counsel found himself in a room with very experienced, intelligent investigators and he had to convince them that Maritza was telling the truth about her role and that they should not oppose her bail. Dunn needed to give the police a piece of evidence to persuade them that he and his client were not wasting the officers' time.

'We can help you with the current investigation.'

Rix responded with little enthusiasm. 'We don't need any help.'

'Well, perhaps we can save you some time and trouble.'

'It's going fine.'

Dunn persevered. 'Let's say our client could give you something to help you, enough to charge her with an offence. You charge her and not oppose her bail. Then, if you decide that she has not been frank with you, you can find her [because she is reporting on bail] and charge her with something more substantial. What say I had instructions like this?'

Dunn went on. 'Matthew hit his mother and stepfather over the back of the head a few times, he stacked their bodies up against the front fence in the dirt, he left them there a day and then buried them. There should be bloodstains in the garden. Let's also say that Matthew came home to get more dirt from his garden and some rocks to put on the grave.'

Now Dunn had the investigators' attention. The police asked the lawyers to leave the room for a moment. When they returned, Rix said, 'You might have something there.'

From that moment, things started happening quickly.

Galbally and Peter Ward, a partner at Galbally's firm of Galbally and O'Bryan and known as a wily strategist in criminal law circles, had had a meeting with Maritza to tell her of the Homicide Squad's position. On 10 May the solicitors had drafted a five-page 'can say' statement in their office and got Maritza to sign it. While a 'can say' statement can't be used as evidence against an accused person, it is a useful summary of the evidence they *could* give in court if required. The solicitors sent a copy of Maritza's statement to the Homicide Squad and made arrangements for Maritza to meet with the investigators. On Saturday 11 May Maritza had a recorded interview with police. In that interview she told them all she knew about the murders on 4 April and the actions of her husband since that date. Matthew knew nothing of the interview until it was over. While his family were laying their mother and stepfather's ashes to rest, Matthew was being arrested for their murders.

CHAPTER 18

Confessing

11 May 2002

AT 8.30 AM ON SATURDAY 11 MAY, THE MEETING ROOM OF THE Homicide Squad was buzzing with excitement. Waddell gathered his crew to brief them on the arrest plan for Matthew Wales. Today was the day. The carefully worked out timetable, which the Homicide Squad had discussed with Dunn and Galbally, was not going to run according to plan. The Homicide Squad detectives had decided to arrest Matthew as soon as possible. There was some concern that he was depressed and that the pressure within his family unit was getting too much. The detectives were worried that Matthew might kill himself.

By 10.18 am, Nazaretian, Fraser, Van Veenendaal and Waddell were in a quiet, residential street in the eastern suburb of Kew where Matthew and Maritza had moved that week to live near her parents. The media swarms and the busybodies hanging around their Burke Road house had become unbearable. Every time one of them stepped out the front gate, a horde of journalists and photographers rushed forward. Their house had been kept under surveillance by the media and the locals. Next door, reporters had set up camp in the neighbours' rambling front garden. They brought ladders and leant against the fence to look down into the Wales's front yard.

Local women dropped their children off at Caulfield Grammar's Malvern campus and then congregated in the wine shop across the road, sharing the round laminated tables with journalists. The women sat and watched Matthew and Maritza's house and, making their coffees last longer than usual, traded gossip about the murders. They all knew someone who knew something about the investigation or the Wales family.

Everyone inside 1/152 Burke Road, Glen Iris was feeling the pressure. Matthew had been depressed and Maritza was worried about him. She had closed her shop and spent her days staying inside with her two-year-old son. Even taking Domenik to the nearby park was impossible; their faces were known and people stared. She felt like a prisoner in a house that she had grown to hate.

In Kew, people still knew who they were but it was quieter and the Pizzaros provided the family with some emotional support.

Matthew was driving east in his red Nissan Patrol when an unmarked police car pulled up behind him with its blue light flashing. He looked in his rear vision mirror and pulled over to the kerb. The moment he had expected since the evening of 4 April had arrived. Waddell and Nazaretian approached the car. Waddell asked Matthew to step out of it. He wasted no time with pleasantries. He too had been waiting for this moment. He gave Matthew the standard arrest caution. 'Matthew, you are under arrest for the murder of Margaret Wales-King and Paul King. You are not obliged to say or do anything but anything you say or do may be given in evidence. Do you understand that?'

Matthew said, 'Yes.'

Detectives Stamper and Donohue pulled up in another unmarked police car. Their job was to arrange for Matthew's car to be transported to the Victorian Forensic Science Centre for examination. Where he was going, he wouldn't be needing it.

By 10.32 am Matthew Wales was sitting in the back seat of the police car with Waddell, Van Veenendaal and Nazaretian. He arrived at the largest police station in Melbourne, the St Kilda Road Police Complex, at 10.45 am. It is only thirteen minutes in a fast car between the leafy opulence of Kew and the utilitarian corridors of the police station, but Matthew Wales had been transported to another world and he knew it.

The detectives put Matthew into a locked interview room on the Homicide Squad floor. A small room without windows, it held three small brown chairs and a chipboard government-issue desk. The beige walls were bare. Once the bulky shapes of Waddell and Van Veenendaal occupied the two chairs opposite Matthew, the room was full. A video camera set in the wall filmed the entire 190 minute interview.

Waddell conducted the interview. Van Veenendaal sat to one side and occasionally asked questions. His role was to corroborate the interview should its contents ever be shown to a jury. Both police officers had short dark hair and moustaches and wore pale cotton shirts with plain ties. Matthew was dressed in black pants and a silky deep purple shirt with an impeccably matching tie. As the interview progressed he took off the tie and rolled it into a neat coil on the desk in front of him. Next to it he placed a gold packet of cigarettes. His pale, shaved head glistened in the fluorescent lights and he kept his dark eyes firmly focused on his interrogator. Matthew spoke well, revealing the diction of a private school education. Throughout the interview his voice was soft and he barely changed his tone or modulation. Without any visible emotion, Matthew spoke of bashing his parents' heads in with a piece of wood. He only stumbled before answering a question, or appeared upset, when he spoke about two things – the effect of his crimes on Maritza and Domenik and his feelings of alienation from his siblings. During the rest of the interview, Matthew was composed and clear. An onlooker, unable to hear what was being spoken of, may have mistaken the interview for a loan application being assessed by two bank managers.

At 11.06 am Waddell began the preliminary part of the interview. He told Matthew that he intended to interview him about the murder of Margaret Wales-King and Paul King. He gave him the legally required caution. 'Before continuing, I must inform you that you are not obliged to say or do anything, but anything you say or do may be given in evidence. Do you understand that?' Matthew did.

Waddell then read Matthew his rights. Known as communication rights, the rights are enshrined in criminal law and must be given to an accused person, and understood by them, before any questions can be asked by police in an interview. Waddell told Matthew that he had the right to call a friend or relative to tell them where he was and the right to speak to, or at least try and speak to, a lawyer. Matthew asked to speak to his solicitor, Steve Pica. At 11.07 am, the interview was suspended so that Matthew could call him.

The interview recommenced at 12.15 pm. Waddell reminded Matthew of the caution and his rights and confirmed that he had spoken to his lawyer. Then the detective started asking questions. He asked Matthew 1469 questions over 190 minutes. Matthew answered every one of them.

Waddell started the interview by getting Matthew to read the first statement that he had made with Waddell on 9 April and explain which bits were false. Then Waddell asked what had really happened after dinner on 4 April 2002. Matthew answered matter-of-factly: '. . . once Maritza went upstairs, Mum and I went outside with Paul, and I hit them with a block of wood on the back of the neck.' He drew diagrams to help his interrogators understand where in the front garden he had killed his mother and stepfather. Matthew sketched the front paving, the grass areas and made two marks to show where his mother and stepfather had lain after he hit them. He marked the spot where he left the bodies beside the fence. He wrote 'BS' for 'bloodstain' where the bodies had seeped blood onto the paving. Matthew drew another picture to explain to the police officers exactly what links were on the chain his mother wore to dinner. He drew a picture of the rounded end of the piece of pine he killed them with.

It didn't take long for Matthew to disclose his motive for the murder of his mother. At question 45, Waddell asked Matthew why he had prepared for the killing. What followed was a series of questions and answers that eventually made its way onto the ABC News 7 pm bulletin on 24 October 2002 and into the lounge room of over four hundred thousand Victorians.

Matthew: Because there's so much animosity and hurt between my mother and myself . . .
Waddell: Explain the animosity to us, Matthew.
Matthew: [Pause] When . . . earlier in – in the piece – and this has been steaming up for a long, long, long time –
Waddell: Okay.
Matthew: Pretty early in . . . – basically, Mum used a lot of h. . . – you want to know the motive behind it? Is that –
Waddell: I want to know the reason, yeah.
Matthew: Everybody will prob'ly think it's about the

money, okay?

Waddell: Okay.

Matthew: And it is about money.

Waddell: Okay.

Matthew: Not for the use of me [sic] getting the money. It's the way she used her – her power for money.

Waddell: Okay.

Matthew: She used it against us all the time. She used it against Sally, she used it against Emma, she used it against Prudence. I'm not too sure about Damian, but she's also used it against me . . .

I just feel that every time she wanted me to do something, like sign papers or whatever, she used to use leverage. Not signing papers, but if I wanted to do something, you know what I mean, and she wanted – she used to use that leverage over us all the time.

Waddell: Okay.

Matthew: As if, you know, basically, 'You're not going to get a will [sic]', and all that type of thing, but it – it – but it wasn't the fact of the money for – for us.

Waddell: Mm'm.

Matthew: It was the fact that she used to use the leverage over us all the time.

Waddell: Okay. Well, we need to go on and do it in a little bit more detail, Matthew.

Matthew: I'm just trying to think. There is more to it than just that. It's not just the money. It's also just the way she used to treat – she used to manipulate us.

Waddell: In what way?

Matthew: It's just like sh–, I feel she's just alienated me from the family, as well. I walked around my sister's house the other day, and I noticed that everybody else's photo was up except for mine.

Waddell: Yep. Was this Sally's house?

Matthew: [Crying] I – I was always of the mind that – they used this – I don't know – just this anger that built up inside me, that they just wanted to alienate me from the family.

After this answer, Matthew cried and hid his head in his hands.

When he had composed himself, Matthew told Waddell that the anger had been building up in him for years, since he was a child, and that he had 'always had that aggression' towards his mother. He repeated that he was alienated from his family and started crying again.

Matthew said that he had not talked with anyone about his plans to kill his mother. He was emphatic that Maritza had no idea what was going on.

He said that a week or two before the dinner, he had thought about murdering his mother when she came over. What triggered it, he told Waddell, was a dispute with his mother over the signing of some paperwork in relation to the sale of a unit in Queensland.

The 30-year old unit on the beachfront in Garfield Terrace, Surfers Paradise, was the only remaining asset of Matthew's grandfather's estate. The income from the unit was paid to two trusts – one for each of Robert Lord's daughters and their children. The terms of Lord's will meant that during the lifetimes of Margaret and Di, their children only shared in the income if the estate trustees considered it 'wise and prudent' to do so after taking into consideration the needs of Margaret and Di. After the sisters' deaths, the half-share in the unit went to their children. In the months before the murders, there had been a family dispute

Despite the families' decision to keep the location of the funeral service a secret, the cameras started rolling when the church doors opened. The media seemed to consider that the grief of the Wales family was public property.

A few days after the funeral, on 11 May 2002, Matthew was arrested for the murder of his mother and stepfather.

Di Yeldham, sister of Margaret Wales-King, leaves the Magistrates Court with one of her nieces on 2 September 2002 after a court appearance by Matthew and Maritza.

On 18 December 2002, Matthew Wales was escorted to the Victorian Supreme Court to face the charge of double murder.

Flanked by Paul Galbally and Phil Dunn QC's junior, Kate Rowe, Maritza Wales leaves the Supreme Court on 11 April 2003, after watching her husband being sentenced for killing his mother and stepfather.

about the proposed sale of the unit. Di Yeldham had wanted to sell the unit since 1997. She wanted to wind up the Yeldham family trust and have the proceeds from the sale paid to her children. Margaret did not want the Wales trust wound up because she didn't want her children to have control of the money.

After a few months of debate between the Lord sisters, their children and the trustees, it was agreed that the unit would be sold privately, a means not approved of under the terms of the trust. The trustees wanted all the beneficiaries of the trust, Di and Margaret and their children, to sign an indemnity to protect the trustees from any legal action in relation to the sale. When the Wales children were told about the proposed sale and the indemnity, they wanted to have a say in it.

On 19 December 2001, Margaret, her daughters and Matthew met at the office of her solicitor, Tony Joyce, to discuss the sale. The sisters wanted to know the particulars of their grandfather's will in relation to the unit. They also wanted to know what Margaret intended to do with her share of the proceeds of the sale. Margaret told her children that she wanted to set up a new trust with herself as the income beneficiary for the rest of her life and with her children inheriting the money when she died. Tony Joyce recalls that Margaret's children didn't like this and wanted to be more involved: 'Margaret told them that would not happen and the meeting concluded in turmoil'.

Matthew was not the only one upset with his mother over the proposed sale. Prudence felt that the new trust suggested by her mother should have at least one of the children on it. 'Our names were on it [the current trust in relation to the unit] for a reason, because Pa left it to us ... She [Margaret] became very angry and said leave it with the trustees. She didn't talk to us for so long, for two weeks for me.'

Sally Honan was relieved to get out of the solicitor's office and away from her mother's anger. 'To be honest, we were pleased that we hadn't been railroaded into something we didn't fully understand because Mum wanted us to sign those papers no matter what and we felt we were being treated like children who didn't understand what was going on.'

Two days after the family meeting, the solicitor sent a letter to the children saying that Margaret had decided to keep the estate income as it was, with a trustee company. In February, Tony Joyce sent a second letter to the Wales siblings asking them to sign a request that the trustees accept an offer of $565 000 for the unit.

On 6 February, Tony Joyce received a call from Matthew asking where the proceeds of the unit would be paid. The solicitor told Matthew that the money would go into a trust and the income would go to his mother. Matthew replied, 'No worries, I will sign it and return it tonight.' He did so. Eventually the five Wales children signed both the indemnity for the trustees and the letter asking the trustees to accept the offer of $565 000. Matthew told Waddell that his mother had not spoken to him for a month over the disagreement about the sale and that it 'just built up from that last point that I had had enough'.

Waddell took Matthew back to the night of 4 April and asked him questions about every step he had taken to prepare for and execute the killings. He asked him about the hours before the murders and about the days after them. He asked about the steps that Matthew took to cover up his crimes and to bury the bodies. Waddell asked Matthew about the meal he had cooked, the conversation they had over dinner, the strikes he had made to his mother's and stepfather's heads and what he had done immediately afterwards. One question Matthew wasn't asked was what he had done with the murder weapon. It was never found.

Matthew told Waddell that after leaving his mother's car locked in Middle Park, he walked south towards St Kilda where he hailed a taxi. The detectives didn't ask Matthew what the taxi driver thought of his bloodied customer. Matthew said that the taxi dropped him close to home and that he paid the driver cash.

Waddell told Matthew what the autopsies had revealed. He asked Matthew to comment on the forensic pathologist's finding of death by asphyxia and his notes that each body had suffered bruising around the neck.

Matthew: That's what I find strange.
Waddell: Would you care to comment on that?
Matthew: Because there was no – there's no strangulisation [sic] at all. No strangling. I hit them on the back of the neck ... It's not true. I'm not saying they're liars. I'm saying I hit them on the back of the neck with a block of wood. I didn't – I didn't torture them at all.

Waddell twice asked Matthew to clarify whether his purpose in hitting Margaret and Paul was to kill them both. Matthew replied: 'Yeah. I had – I had in mind to destroy their life because – there's many becauses and many reasons.'

Despite his clear motivation to kill, Matthew told the detective that he had some ambiguity about executing his plan on the night. 'I was scared, because at the end of the day – not at the end but during the procedure of the night, I – I changed my mind, but my – my instincts went and did it ... What made me turn was because I had gave them – given them those pills.'

More than once Waddell asked whether Matthew had acted alone. Matthew cried when the detective asked him that. He stared his interrogator in the eyes and said: 'Maritza had nothing to do with this at all. This is me. This is my emotions that went out and then –'.

Towards the end of the interview Waddell asked Matthew to explain what his motive was in killing Paul King. Matthew told the two detectives: 'I quite like Paul, but at the same time he – he destroyed my mother's and father's relationship too.' Matthew did not tell the detectives what he had seen Paul do in the toy room on the night of the murders or about the sexual abuse he had suffered as a child.

After answering 1467 questions, Matthew agreed to give his fingerprints to police. At 3.25 pm the interview concluded with two charges of murder and a request from Matthew for a cup of tea – white and one sugar.

*

At 5.30 pm, Van Veenendaal and Waddell took Matthew in an unmarked police car to the Melbourne Magistrates' Court in the city. An out of sessions court was constituted before a bail justice and Matthew made his first appearance as an accused person. The court was held in a small room within the court building. Squeezed into it were four of the Homicide Squad detectives and two uniformed protective services officers, the security guards of the court. Eight members of the media, three more than the court originally allowed, were standing in one corner of the room, furiously scribbling notes during the hearing. Detective Van Veenendaal told the bail justice the outline of the case against Matthew Robert Wales, emphasising the fact that he had made full admissions during his interview. The bail justice, a middle-aged man who had been on call for the night, heard what the detective had to say and made an order refusing Matthew bail and remanding him in custody to appear at the Melbourne Magistrates' Court on the next business day, Monday 13 May.

One of the protective services officers took Matthew through a door in the side of the room and out of his normal world. He was lodged in a single, bare cell below the court to wait for his next court appearance. The next morning when Matthew woke up after his first night in custody, it was Sunday 12 May – Mother's Day.

*

Twenty minutes after her husband was arrested in their street, Maritza arrived at the car park at the bottom of the police complex. She did so voluntarily. At 11.08 am Detective Senior Constables Narelle Fraser and Robert Nazaretian took her into custody in an interview room.

At 12.30 pm, the interview of Maritza Elizabeth Wales commenced. Nazaretian asked her 794 questions in an interview that stopped and started and didn't finish until 6.55 pm. Fraser corroborated the interview. Maritza was read the same caution, about anything she said being used as evidence against her, and the same communication rights as Matthew. She agreed that she had already had legal advice and was attending the Homicide Squad offices of her own accord. Maritza whispered her answers to the first few preliminary questions. She sat in a chair opposite Nazaretian. He was young and handsome, dark-haired and olive-skinned in a light blue shirt. Maritza wore a denim jacket, tight jeans and lots of gold jewellery and, after her reticence at the beginning of the interview, smiled and laughed with her interrogators. By the end she was crying and pleading, telling them that she did not do anything to help Matthew. She wore her hair, the curly hair that had started her friendship with Matthew, pulled back off her face. Throughout the interview she clasped a white tissue in her hands and rubbed at her eyes and scratched her head. Maritza had aged in the last few weeks. Her eyes were ringed with dark purple shadows and two new furrows made their way from either side of her nose to her mouth. There was little sign of the sex kitten her sister-in-laws had described.

Nazaretian started the interview by showing Maritza the statement she made to Detective Shiell in her shop on 9 April. She agreed that the statement was 'not all true'.

She asked the officers if they wanted her to tell them what happened after her family ate dinner with Margaret and Paul. The detectives had been waiting a month to hear the truth. They answered with a resounding 'yes'. Maritza began a narrative which took half an hour to finish. She told her story of the night of 4 April. The police officers didn't interrupt. They listened while she told it all in a rush, as if it were a relief to finally unburden herself.

Maritza's description of the evening prior to the murders was similar to her husband's version of events. She said that she had taken Domenik to bed and then came downstairs to find everybody gone. She went outside and was confronted by the bodies of Margaret and Paul. Matthew, in a frantic state, pushed her inside. She described the next few days as a sleepless blur of tears and migraines and of her trying to go to work and feeling sick. She said that during this time, Matthew kept asking her if she still loved him. She told her interrogators that when the bodies were found in the grave she had pleaded with Matthew to go to the police. Maritza said that since the killings, she couldn't bear to look the Wales sisters in the eye.

At 1.02 pm Nazaretian stopped Maritza, saying that 'based on what you've just told us, we have a number of inquiries to now make'.

The interview was restarted at 4.13 pm. Nazaretian began by asking Maritza how she first met Matthew. She told the detective about the friendship with her hairdresser that quickly led to a romance. In the middle of describing their early courtship days, Maritza said with a giggle, 'It sounds like a love story.' She told her interrogators that: 'We've always been close. Always been, like – it was, like Matthew was my first boyfriend I ever had. I never had a boyfriend before.' She said that Matthew was her closest friend.

Throughout the interview, Maritza was asked many questions about her and Matthew's financial affairs. She told them that she knew nothing about their finances, not even their pin numbers for their bankcards. She said that Matthew was in charge of all that. She told police that she knew Matthew owned the house the couple had first lived in, at 6 Horace Street, Malvern, with his mother through a trust. Maritza referred to Margaret as 'Mum' and said that Margaret called her 'Ritzy'. Maritza thought Matthew received about $70 000 when the house was sold and then, later on, another $70 000 after a fight with his mother over the remaining sum.

In answer to a question from Nazaretian about the cash in their accounts and the family's income, Maritza apologised to her interrogators. 'Sorry. I'm really hopeless at this . . . The financial thing. I don't know. I don't know.' Matthew paid all the bills. Maritza agreed that they paid about $1900 a month rent for the townhouse in Burke Road, they owed money on their car, a boat which had since been sold and a television. She described their financial position as sometimes a bit tight and sometimes okay. She could recall that they had borrowed money from her brother, Mario, to get her 'boobies done'. After many questions about money matters, which Maritza could not answer, Nazaretian moved to Maritza's relationship with Margaret and Paul.

Maritza described her relationship with her mother-in-law as 'fine'. She said that she had never had an argument with her but that when Matthew and Margaret fought, her mother-in-law would not call their house. Maritza said that Margaret would pop into her shop when she was in High Street and bring her hot drinks. 'She used to spend money in the shop but she was just helping us . . . She used to buy a scarf . . . because I only do size 6 to size 12 and mum's about, like, size 14. So a lot of things didn't fit her – she tried to fit into them, like a couple of jackets she bought and they were a bit fitted for her but she still bought them.' Maritza felt that her mother-in-law was a snob and sometimes she could be 'a real bitch'. When asked how this showed itself, Maritza replied: 'Whenever she got upset with the kids, she never used to talk to them and things like that, you know, for – for a week, two weeks and stuff like that and – and things like that and I thought she was a little bit mean with Paul too, the way she used to treat him.' Maritza said that generally she liked her mother-in-law. Whether the feeling was mutual, she didn't know. She told the detectives that Margaret used to say that she was 'a bit too fussy' with Domenik.

Nazaretian asked Maritza what her perceptions were of her husband's relationship with his mother. Maritza said: 'Sometimes they used to get on each other's horses . . . Matt sometimes used to get upset with his mum and . . . none of them would budge.' Maritza told the detectives that her husband used to complain that his mother never gave him much help compared with the assistance she gave his sisters. She thought that Matthew resented his mother and felt that she treated Domenik differently from the other grandchildren, although Maritza said that Margaret used to love her grandson, Domenik, and that Paul was really good with the child.

Maritza saw none of this conflict between Matthew and Paul. She found Paul to be gentle, never saying much at all. She said it was like he wasn't there. As for the rest of the Wales family,

Maritza said that she 'got on with them fine' despite not seeing them much. Maritza explained to the detectives that she had a different life from her sisters-in-laws because, unlike them, she worked and didn't pay for long hours of babysitting to socialise.

Maritza told the detectives that Matthew was not close to his brother, Damian, and never had been and that he used to tell her that his sister Sally 'hated his guts'. Of the sisters, Matthew used to get on best with Emma and Prue but Maritza didn't describe those relationships as very close either. She said that Matthew felt left out of his family.

From her observations, Maritza felt that Margaret and Paul had a relationship where Paul did everything for his wife. Once Paul got sick, Maritza said, even her daughters didn't like the way Margaret treated him. Maritza never saw the couple hugging. Maritza told her interrogators that she didn't know much about her in-laws' wealth or the relative incomes of Matthew's siblings. She thought that they were all in a different position from her and Matthew because they were financially established. Maritza told Nazaretian that the Wales sisters all seemed to be doing 'pretty well'. She said, 'They've all got houses and things like that and – and we don't own a house, not yet anyway, but – it's different ... Matthew and I, we're just starting. The other girls have been divorced and everything, you know. We're just starting our life.'

Nazaretian then asked Maritza a series of questions about the events of 4 April. She answered them all. She told him that Matthew always did the family cooking and that his mood had seemed fine during the dinner. She said that the first thing she knew about the murders was when she saw the bodies of Margaret and Paul lying on the ground outside her front door. She said that she thought they were dead but didn't know because Matthew pushed her inside very quickly. Her interviewers didn't ask her whether she checked if they were alive or not. Maritza told Nazaretian that it felt like a bad dream.

> I was feeling sick and I started to cry and – and Matthew was white. I remember he was just white and – and pale and he was shaking and all sweaty and then he said to me – he said to me 'I had to do it. I feel like a relief . . . I had it in me. I had to. I had to,' he said. 'I had it in me,' and that was it.

After the murders had been committed, Maritza had been upset and vomited on the stairs. She asked her husband what he was going to do. She cried as she told Nazaretian, 'I just didn't want to know. I just wanted to rub it out of my head but then this turned into a nightmare . . . Since this, I just been sick. I feel like my whole life has just been turned.' Maritza returned to this theme later in the interview:

> I couldn't believe how it happened. I just – I don't got any feelings at the moment at all. Nothing. Since this thing happened, I've got nothing, nothing. All my life – my life has just been turned, switched and all I want to do, to tell the truth is . . . to die. If I had a gun, I shoot myself. I just want to die. I love my boy but I don't think I can handle all this pressure and the bullshit. I can't handle it anymore. I was – it was family, my good family. I just want to die. I'm so tired. It's just like a nightmare. I wake up in the morning, I just want it to go away. I just want it to go away. I want to get back to normal. I can't even take Domenik to the park when people are staring, taking photos and shit like that. I can't handle it anymore.

Maritza said that she pleaded with Matthew to go to the police and confess once the bodies were found. She told her husband that he was putting Domenik through hell. He replied that he wouldn't confess yet because he wanted to spend more time with her and Domenik. She thought that Matthew was really depressed at this time. When she raised the question of him confessing, he begged her: 'Please, Maritza, please don't dob me in.' Maritza said that despite her husband's pleading, she went to see her solicitor because she couldn't stand it anymore and she was also 'scared for Matt because I don't know what Matt might do'. Maritza was not asked why she had her own solicitor and did not use Matthew's.

Nazaretian asked Maritza why she didn't get any help for Margaret and Paul. She replied that she 'didn't want to know. I didn't want to touch anything. Didn't want to know what happened. Nothing. I didn't want to know why he did it. I didn't want to. I was scared. I know what Matthew has done was wrong but I was scared.'

The detective then asked Maritza why she didn't tell the police what happened. She replied: 'Because I was thinking of Domenik. I was thinking of Matt. I was thinking of everything except for . . . the right thing.'

When asked why she supplied a false statement to police, Maritza started crying and said that Matthew had told her to. She was scared. 'Scared of losing Matt. Scared of losing Domenik. Just – I feel like I'm pulled from left, right and centre. I didn't know what to do.'

After 769 questions, Nazaretian had heard enough to lay formal charges against Maritza. He told her that she was suspected of being an accessory to the murders. Finally Maritza went to pieces. Until then she had generally maintained her composure.

She pleaded with him, 'I didn't do anything. I didn't – Robert, I didn't know anything that happened. I did nothing. Nothing, nothing. Robert – I swear to God. I didn't help Matthew to do anything. Just because he told me to lie about that. I was, like, scared. I didn't know what to do. I didn't know where to go from here or there.' Matthew had told her that if she told police the truth, he would go to jail.

Nazaretian explained that the basis of the charge against her was her false statement to police on 9 April. He then told Maritza that she was going to be charged with being an accessory to the murder of Margaret Wales and Paul King.

Maritza shook her head and slumped back in her chair, defeated.

She consented to giving her fingerprints and a mouth swab for DNA analysis. At 6.55 pm, nearly eight hours after her arrival at the police complex, the interview was over.

Maritza was charged and released on bail to appear in the Melbourne Magistrates' Court, with Matthew, on the following Monday. The next day, while crowds watched, the police were digging up her front yard in Glen Iris. She spent Mother's Day with her son and without her husband.

Part Six

Prosecuting

Give me your blessing, truth will come to light;
murder cannot be hid long;
a man's son may be, but in the end truth will out.

Shakespeare, *The Merchant of Venice*, Act 2, Scene 2

CHAPTER 19

Analysing

29 May – 4 December 2002

IAN JOBLIN, FORENSIC PSYCHOLOGIST, WORKS FROM A SMALL, dishevelled office in an art deco building in the low rent part of Queen Street, Melbourne. In many senses he is a long way from where he started his career, in the quiet university town of Palmerston North in New Zealand, but Joblin has been in the courtrooms of Melbourne giving evidence for criminals for twenty-five years. In an office filled with thick textbooks leaning on brown laminated shelves, a creeping potato vine growing out of a plastic pot and a print of Lake Horowhenua in 1875, Joblin sees the side of society many like to put out of their minds. Nearly 15 000 clients later, Joblin still loves his job.

Joblin makes house calls, not always by choice. A lot of Joblin's clients miss the chance to read the magazines in his miniature waiting room or see the view out of his open window – they are in prison. He goes to the 'big house' as many times as he has to in order to work out what makes the accused person tick and to discover what is going on in their minds. Joblin visits until he can make some sense of his client even if he has to do so for free. After the legal aid funding has run out, Joblin keeps paying visits until he can finish the story, write his court report and go home to his alpaca farm.

It took Joblin nine trips until he worked out Matthew Robert Wales's mind. Nine one-hour sessions at Port Phillip Prison in Laverton, a suburb on the ugly western edge of Melbourne, and Joblin was confident he could write a report that would help a Supreme Court judge decide what to do with him. Joblin first saw Matthew on 29 May and paid his last official visit on 4 December 2002. He had been asked to see Matthew by Wales's solicitor, Steve Pica. Pica ran his own show, Clareborough Pica, and had been knocking around the criminal law for years. Joblin's brief was to see Matthew, assess his mental state and then prepare a report that would be filed on the day of the plea hearing. The forensic psychologist would then give sworn evidence in court on Matthew's behalf.

Joblin's first impression of Matthew was that he was 'not right'. He couldn't put his finger on what was wrong with him but he knew that his client wasn't mad or, as they call it these days, 'mentally impaired'. Joblin knew better than to use the nature of Matthew's crimes to determine his client's mental state. He couldn't find any diagnosis for Matthew's 'not rightness' in the list of all known mental illnesses contained in the forensic psychologists' bible, the DSM IV Manual.

Joblin administered eleven psychological tests to work out his client's IQ. Six of the tests rated Matthew's verbal capacity and five looked at his performance abilities with various mental tasks. Matthew did the tests. Joblin did the maths and came up with a score of 83. Matthew's IQ placed him in the bottom 12.9 per cent of a community of his peers. That meant that 87.1 per cent of people in Matthew's age group would score higher than he did and only 12.8 per cent would do worse. The score also indicated that Matthew fell into the 'low average intelligence' classification for his age. Considering that an average IQ is 90 to 109, 120 plus is a Mensa candidate and below 80 is virtually non-functioning; Matthew's IQ indicated to Joblin that his client's intelligence was quite limited and that his abstract reasoning was not highly developed.

Joblin put Matthew through as many neuropsychological tests as the time limits and resources in Port Phillip Prison would allow. Matthew tried his hand at the Trail Making Tests, the Aphasia Screening Test and the Finger Tapping Test. Designed to assess a person's recognition of sequences in numbers and letters, language abilities and motor skills, Matthew either could not complete or scored poorly on almost all the tests. Joblin found that the pattern of Matthew's scores indicated that it was highly likely that Matthew suffered from dyslexia. Certainly, Matthew's school performance supported Joblin's diagnosis.

The tests showed something else that troubled the forensic psychologist. The scores were puzzling and indicated scattered brain functioning. Joblin thought that Matthew might have an undiagnosed organic brain impairment. Certainly, he felt that the randomness of the results was significant enough to warrant some further neurological assessment.

In an ideal world, Joblin would have sent Matthew off for a Magnetic Resonance Imaging (MRI) scan or a CT scan on his brain. Unfortunately, Port Phillip Prison is as far from the ideal world as anyone can get and Joblin realised pretty quickly that his client was not going to get the tests he wanted. Matthew would have to pay for the tests and, despite his family's wealth, he was broke and on legal aid funding. The Legal Aid Commission of Victoria's grant of aid would not stretch to paying for a neurologist, expensive tests and the necessary escorts to ensure that

Matthew travelled safely outside the prison to have the tests and remembered to come back. No money meant no tests. Despite a niggling feeling that the brain scans might tell him more, Joblin had to rely on Matthew's presentation and the results of his psychological tests to write the court report.

In the Victorian criminal justice system, a registered psychologist who examines a person awaiting trial must determine the question of whether that person is 'fit to plead'. The *Crimes (Mental Impairment and Unfitness to be Tried) Act* sets out the criteria to be applied by a psychologist when making the determination. By law, Joblin was required to look at whether Matthew's mental processes were disordered to such a degree that he would be unable to understand the nature of the charges against him or follow the legal proceedings.

It was obvious that Matthew was fit to plead. Joblin realised immediately that Matthew was not mad and that he was capable of giving instructions to his lawyers about what he wanted to do in court. Joblin found his client to be a forthcoming but extremely suspicious young man. Despite his suspicious nature, Matthew responded to Joblin's relaxed, straight talking manner and opened up to him. He told Joblin that he felt extremely isolated and lonely in prison.

During the seven months Joblin saw him, Matthew had not been visited by any of his siblings. The only contact he'd had with his family was one forty-minute visit with his father, Brian Wales, in late May and one with his stepfather's brother, Father Stephen King, in the last week of June. Matthew told Joblin that his sister closest to him in age, Prudence Reed, had written him a letter in prison. Excitedly opening it, Matthew had been shattered to read the pages of abuse she had sent him.

Throughout their sessions, Joblin asked his client about his relationship with his wife. Joblin had interviewed Maritza Wales as part of the preparation of his court report. Maritza had not been to see Matthew in prison. She spoke to him on the telephone as often as she was allowed to and had seen him briefly in court. Although Maritza was on bail from the day she was arrested, she could not visit the prison to see her husband. Prison access is prohibited between two people accused of the same crime, until they have both been sentenced, in case they conspire to change their evidence.

Domenik was free to see his father during visiting hours. With Maritza banned from the prison by virtue of her status as a co-offender, and the Wales family shunning Matthew's wife and child, the only way Matthew could see his son was if his in-laws brought him to the prison. The Pizzaros have a poor level of English and are not the sort of people to be comfortable around authority figures such as prison guards. Unassertive and linguistically disadvantaged, 71-year-old Mario Pizzaro, Maritza's father, took his two-year-old grandson on the two-hour round trip from Kew to Port Phillip Prison in Laverton many times. Joblin heard how the grandfather had waited with the toddler for up to three hours in the visitors' waiting lounge before Matthew was brought in from his cell for a visit. Matthew told Joblin that the one bright spot in his otherwise bleak future was thinking of the day when he could sit with his wife and son in the prison visiting area and have a normal conversation with them.

Joblin discovered that Matthew was feeling deeply disappointed with his brother and sisters. He had shown Matthew the many newspaper stories published about his crimes. Matthew read the comments made by his family in the media. He read that they wanted Maritza prosecuted for murder for not helping Margaret and Paul after the attack, that they couldn't believe

Matthew had committed the murders alone and that they thought his claims that their mother was a manipulative power-broker were groundless. Matthew told Joblin that he found it disappointing that his brother and sisters rejected that he had any problems with their mother. He could not fathom that they did not understand his point of view or share it. He thought that once he had killed their mother, his siblings would share his sense of absolute relief that she was gone.

Joblin is clear that he saw no hint that Matthew harboured any desire to kill any other members of his family or anyone else. He found that while Matthew did not understand abstract concepts, such as others' perceptions, he was not aggressive about people who did not share his views. He thought it unlikely that Matthew would develop an obsessional hatred of any of his siblings.

The forensic psychologist does not believe that Maritza manipulated Matthew to kill his parents. Over the seven months he visited Matthew, Joblin realised that his client had a drive to take the lives of his mother and stepfather that had coalesced into an obsession. Joblin believed that the drive was founded in the profound psychological distress Matthew felt about his relationships with his mother and stepfather. He believes that it was solely Matthew's obsession with the hurt they had caused him that led him to murder them. He found that his client had, and continues to have despite the adverse circumstances, a strong, positive emotional relationship with Maritza. Joblin remains impressed with Maritza's continued support of her husband and her intelligence. He believes that the obsessive nature of Matthew's love for Maritza deepened the more isolated he became from the rest of his family.

Joblin commented later that if the Wales siblings had recognised that their brother had a difficult relationship with their mother then there could have been a different outcome to Matthew's story. As it was, Matthew told Joblin that since he was a little boy he had been pushed further and further away from the family. He felt that he, Maritza and Domenik were alienated from the others.

Matthew gave Joblin many examples of the poor treatment he had received from his mother. At one session with the forensic psychologist, Matthew handed over eight handwritten pages detailing some of the issues he had with Margaret. Joblin quizzed him about each one. Joblin was struck by the intensity of the feelings that Matthew had about his mother. Matthew believed that his mother had dominated him emotionally, physically and financially all his life. He told of a history of psychological abuse and cruelty, exclusion and manipulation by a mother who was domineering and controlling in every aspect of her son's life. In Matthew's mind, the only way around the pain his mother had caused him was to remove her from his life.

Two examples of his mother's cruelty towards him that Matthew shared with Joblin stayed with the psychologist months after he had finished the court reports. Matthew said that at one stage after the birth of their son, he and Maritza had wanted to move to Spain to start a new life. Margaret withdrew permission to use the proceeds of the sale of the house in Horace Street, Malvern, in such a way that it thwarted the couple's plan.

Matthew told Joblin that one Christmas Maritza had made a special effort to find a gift for her mother-in-law. After searching for a while, she eventually bought a set of placemats with a Spanish theme. According to Matthew, Margaret returned the Christmas present, saying that she did not like it.

Matthew told the forensic psychologist that his mother did not approve of Maritza, considering her family 'just wogs' and that they didn't do things like 'we do'. Joblin's conclusion was that the ill treatment that Matthew perceived his mother inflicted on him was 'not a fantasy or [the result of] a deluded state. There is some basis for his grievances. The siblings agree in their statements'.

Matthew told Joblin that he did not kill Paul King simply because he was there. He regarded his stepfather as an extension of his mother and therefore a problem that had to be eliminated with her. He also told Joblin that he had suffered sexual abuse at the hands of his stepfather. The abuse had started when Matthew was about eight or nine, soon after his parents' separation. Margaret had kept Matthew with her and Paul while his brother and sisters spent the weekends staying with their father. Often on those weekends, Matthew had been sent to Paul's farm in Kyneton to spend time with his new stepfather. Matthew says that during these visits, Paul King fondled his genitals. After about three years, Matthew gathered the courage to tell Paul to stop touching him and the abuse stopped.

Because Matthew spoke of always feeling driven to rid himself of his mother and stepfather, Joblin wanted to understand why Matthew had chosen the night of 4 April 2002 to kill them. By that night, Matthew's obsession had been years in the brewing. Matthew told the psychologist that on that evening an incident had occurred which had galvanised him into action. Before dinner was served, Paul King was in the toy room playing with Domenik. Matthew had gone to find them and found his stepfather with his hand at the back of the boy's nappy. While he had thought about killing Margaret and Paul for years, that sight crystallised his thoughts and half-laid plans into action. There was no choice. Matthew returned to the kitchen and added the poison to his guests' soup.

Joblin describes his role in simple terms. 'I see people until I understand what made them do it and then I put the criminal behaviour into the context of their lives.' In Matthew Robert Wales, Joblin found a 34-year-old man of low average intelligence, who may have had an undiagnosed organic brain impairment, who was almost certainly dyslexic and whose motivation to kill his mother and stepfather was simple. He wanted independence from his mother and freedom from the psychological harm he had suffered because of her and his stepfather's actions. 'The drive to eliminate them from his life was so great that it caused him to perceive that he had no alternative but to kill them. The only way he felt he could be free of the suffering was to remove the cause of it.'

Joblin did not find a psychopath who killed for the sake of killing or for no reason. Matthew had his reasons to kill and they made sense to him. Joblin described his client as a person who was psychologically satisfied after removing an issue that had plagued him for most of his life. Having killed his mother and stepfather, Joblin felt that Matthew had neither the desire nor the need to kill again.

Matthew had planned the killing for years. He had fashioned nooses out of pieces of rope, he had sharpened sticks and he had thought about his mother and stepfather's deaths until it became an overriding obsession. On 4 April 2002, Matthew's obsession was laid to rest when he brought the piece of wood down on the backs of their necks.

CHAPTER 20

Prosecuting

11 May – 18 December 2002

ON MONDAY 13 MAY, THE MELBOURNE MAGISTRATES' COURT, a new purpose-built complex in the centre of the city, was busy. Court 1, the mention court, was the largest and busiest court in the building. The first morning of the week was always full with the wash-up from the weekend. Saturday night fighters jostled with the shoplifters, the burglars and the drug addicts for legal attention. Hassled lawyers and defendants milled around the court clerk trying to get some sense of where their case was in the melee. On that Monday, the energy in Court 1 was vibrating at a higher frequency than usual. A score of journalists and a bunch of stickybeaks, had joined the mix and were waiting to see the first court appearance of Matthew and Maritza. Matthew's family was not in the audience. The two detectives who had conducted the interviews of Matthew and Maritza, Van Veenendaal and Nazaretian, were in court as their informants.

Chief Magistrate Ian Gray was sitting on the bench. A gentle compassionate man in his mid-fifties with faded movie star looks, Gray had spent years in the Northern Territory as Chief Magistrate before resigning in protest over the imposition of mandatory sentencing. He brought to the Melbourne Magistrates' Court a steady manner, a kind heart and a sharp mind.

The purpose of the first court date was simply to have the case mentioned to ensure that the defendants were entered into the court system and to set a timetable for the next, more substantive court appearances. Matthew Wales was brought up from the cells to meet with his solicitor, Steve Pica.

The prosecutor, Luisa Dipietrantonio, a solicitor known as 'Dipper' from the Office of Public Prosecutions, asked Gray to make an order that 'no inappropriate media comment be made in this matter until the proceedings are concluded'.

Paul Galbally was in court for Maritza Wales. Gray heard from him and remanded Maritza, on bail, to return to the Magistrates' Court on 2 September 2002 for a further mention of her case. Maritza's bail had special conditions that she report to Kew police station every Monday, Wednesday and Friday, stay living where she was and surrender her passport to the court. Galbally asked for Maritza's address to be kept secret because of the 'unprecedented media attention' in her case. Gray agreed.

Because Matthew was facing two charges of murder, Steve Pica didn't bother asking for bail. He knew he wouldn't get it and that any time his client spent in custody before his case was heard would count towards his final sentence. Pica did ask that his client be moved to a proper prison straight away. He said that the publicity of the case had led to Matthew being held 'in unenviable circumstances' in the holding cells. Pica told Gray that his client had 'achieved a level of notoriety that is really unhealthy for the administration of justice in this state' and that he would have no chance of a fair trial in Victoria.

Gray made a note on the court file that Matthew should be sent to the Melbourne Assessment Prison (MAP), a few blocks away in Spencer Street, as soon as possible. Although Gray had no power to tell the prison system what to do, he knew that the conditions in the jail were better than those in the holding cells below the court. Once Matthew was moved to MAP his mental condition could be assessed and he would be transferred to an appropriate unit in Port Phillip Prison.

Legally, Matthew and Maritza's appearances that morning were short, taking twelve minutes, and straightforward. Nevertheless, the sight of them in court triggered an avalanche of media reports.

Matthew was moved to the Marlborough Unit in Port Phillip Prison, for prisoners who would have difficulty fitting in to the mainstream prison. He had two visitors during his first month in jail. His father was the first, on the morning of 29 May. After waiting for nearly an hour, Brian Wales was led to the visitors' room. Matthew came in. He had lost weight already and was smiling and confident. The father and son hugged each other and sat down at a table. Brian told Matthew that he didn't believe everything that had been reported in the papers.

'I think the whole truth will come out in the long run. Maybe in the trial.'

'Dad, there isn't going to be a trial. I am going to plead guilty.'

'Well, it's a mystery to me, what motive could you have to do such an act?'

'It's clear to me, just utter hatred of the couple. I've had it for the past eight years. The girls hated Mum too.'

Brian Wales was nonplussed. 'I can see from time to time, because of the family trusts and suchlike, you all had some sort of disagreement with your mother, but not this – never savage hatred and wishing her or her husband dead.'

'Dad, money's got nothing to do with it.'

Brian asked Matthew if he had any idea what sort of grief he had caused the whole family.

'Dad, my grief goes back eight years. I don't have any feelings for the rest of them. No one else in the family had the guts to do it.'

After forty minutes, Brian had heard enough; he got up to go. He was disgusted that Matthew thought that he was a hero and that he had done the family a favour by killing Margaret and Paul. He will probably never see his youngest son again.

The second visitor was equally unimpressed with Matthew's demeanour. Father Stephen King had felt it was his duty to see his brother's killer before he returned to Sydney. As a priest he was used to dealing with hardships and finding paths to forgiveness. The difference was this time they were his own. He saw Matthew in prison on the morning of Saturday 22 June. When he arrived in the visitors' room, Matthew told him straight away that he was pleased to see him. He told Stephen that he was sorry about what he had done to him and his other brother and sister. He also told him that he had no remorse about killing Paul and Margaret. Matthew told the priest that his only remorse was for the effect of his actions on his wife and son. Before Stephen left, Matthew told him that he would write him a long letter explaining the whole situation and the truth of what he was experiencing at the time he committed the murders. The priest went back to Sydney under the impression that Matthew had liked and respected his brother. He had a funny way of showing it.

On 2 September, Matthew and Maritza were back in court in front of Chief Magistrate Gray. The cases against the couple were listed for a further mention. The court required a check-in to ensure that the cases were progressing as they should and would be ready for a committal hearing later in the year. This time, the

Wales family had come to court to see their brother and sister-in-law as defendants. Matthew's brother and sisters sat behind Maritza with their aunt, Di Yeldham, and their father.

Maritza had Phil Dunn QC batting for her this time. Matthew had Steve Pica. Prosecutor Dipietrantonio told the Chief Magistrate that the briefs against the two defendants were still being finalised. She also said that the charges against Maritza would be changed from two counts of 'accessory after the fact to murder' to one count of 'attempting to pervert the course of justice'. The mention only took a few minutes. At the end of it, Maritza had her bail changed so that she could report to a more convenient police station. Both defendants were then remanded, Matthew in custody and Maritza to appear back at the court for their joint committal hearing on 17 October 2002.

A committal hearing is held in the Magistrates' Court to decide whether there is a sufficiently strong police case against the defendants to justify it being sent to a higher court for trial. If there isn't, the case is dismissed. If there is, the case continues in the County or Supreme Court on a future date.

Any hopes the participants had of the media attention waning were dashed on 17 October. The court that day was packed with reporters, nosy lawyers, members of the public and the Wales family. Magistrate Barbara Cotterell was assigned the committal hearings. An attractive Italo-phile with long blonde hair and a penchant for fashion, Cotterell is an experienced magistrate who doesn't suffer fools gladly.

The first thing the prosecutor had to do was some house-keeping in relation to Maritza's charges. The two charges of accessory after the fact to murder, one each for Margaret and Paul, were formally withdrawn and the charge of 'attempting to pervert the course of justice by making a false statement on 9 April

2002' was substituted. Maritza's charges were changed because the Homicide Squad detectives had charged Maritza with the wrong offences. A little known provision of the *Crimes Act*, section 338, prevents a married person from being charged as an accessory to a serious crime where all they have done is comfort their spouse after he or she has committed the crime. If the evidence in the police brief, now compiled into 755 pages of statements called 'depositions', had shown that Maritza knew about Matthew's intention to kill his parents before he did so and had helped him do it, her marriage to him would not have prevented her from also being charged with murder. The new charge against Maritza was one of 'attempting to pervert the course of justice', an old common law offence which meant that she had done an act, giving a false statement, and had intended by her act to mislead the police investigating her in-laws' disappearance and possible murder.

While the correct charges were being typed into the magistrate's computer, the Wales sisters grew distressed and held on to each other. Matthew looked towards Maritza. Even though she studiously avoided his eyes, he mouthed 'I love you' across the courtroom.

Through their lawyers, Matthew and Maritza told the magistrate that they wished to plead guilty to the charges against them, making the committal hearing unnecessary. Cotterell had both defendants stand up and formally enter their pleas before the court. Damian Wales shook his fist at his brother and sister-in-law and mouthed curses which the formal atmosphere of the courtroom prevented him from screaming out loud. Cotterell ignored him. She read out the continuing bail conditions for Maritza. Prue couldn't stand it any longer. She leaned towards her sister-in-law and hissed in a stage whisper, 'You fucking rot in hell, whore.' Cotterell continued doing her job. She directed Matthew and Maritza Wales to appear before the Supreme Court on 18 December.

Matthew was taken out the back door of the courtroom to prison. Maritza left the court with Galbally. Outside the courtroom door, Prue rushed up to Maritza and bumped her. Galbally hurried his client into a court interview room and shut the door. Damian Wales kicked the door before being subdued by his sisters. The reporters watched every reaction and reported it in great detail over the next few days. While there are no etiquette books covering the correct way to behave towards your brother and his wife after he has pleaded guilty to your mother's murder, the media obviously felt that the way the Wales family had reacted was worth reporting.

The case remained newsworthy during the rest of October, November and up until the plea hearing. The Wales family's press interviews kept the public's attention aroused during the hiatus in legal proceedings. Sally Honan gave an interview that was published in the *Sunday Age* on 20 October. She said that Matthew was lying about their mother being manipulative and that her family was loving and supportive. Sally blamed greed for her brother's actions, saying, 'I think it's grabbing at anything. See, they're desperate. It was over money – of course it's over money, total greed.' Sally spoke of her sister-in-law as being equally involved as her brother in the murders, commenting that 'Desperate people take desperate measures and we're talking desperate people, financially, emotionally, every which way. And something didn't come off, and Mum and Paul were found. It's short and to the point, isn't it?'

Damian defended his mother in an interview with *Who Weekly* magazine on 4 November. He was quoted as saying that his brother had 'done a lot of harm. He's denigrated my mother's name. Every single step we've taken, he's just kicked us in the teeth. We're just absolutely disgusted with him and I wish I could write him out of my life. It wasn't enough murdering my mother, it's the way he's conducted himself and the lies he's telling in his statement to police . . . There is a lot more to it'.

If that wasn't enough to keep the public panting for more, on 5 December there was a headline that rocked Melbourne and ensured the case would never fade from view. 'Brutally bashed Margaret Wales-King may have been ALIVE FOR SIX HOURS' screamed the headline on the front page of the *Herald Sun* newspaper. The accompanying article, written by radio broadcaster Neil Mitchell, described the conclusion in Dr Dodd's autopsy report that Margaret and Paul may have died from asphyxiation. Mitchell also referred to the couple being left in a garden bed filled with mulch even though Matthew created the garden bed after he had buried his victims. Mitchell reported that the Wales family had been told that their mother might have lived for as long as six hours after the attack. In his report, Dr Dodd did not comment on the time that it would have taken Margaret and Paul to die from their injuries. Rather, he said that they did not die immediately and were probably unconscious after the attack. The Wales family had paid for a private forensic pathologist, Dr Byron Collins, to review Dr Dodd's autopsy, the toxicology results and tissue sample slides.

Mitchell also referred to Dodd's comment that there were signs of strangulation and that Matthew had denied this in his statement to police. Mitchell drew the conclusion that 'The report means that the Wales-King couple may have survived if Matthew's wife, Maritza, had called police after her husband told her he had killed them and left to dump their car in Middle Park

... Family members are concerned that many of the questions surrounding the deaths will never be answered because both have pleaded guilty.'

Sally's husband, Damian Honan, issued a statement on behalf of the family which responded to the autopsy report. Mitchell quoted from it. 'The family recently became aware of this distressing new development. There are other matters which we are also now aware of that we are seeking answers and explanations to. Our great hope is that these matters can be resolved quickly and that we can take one step forward in our lives no matter how short that step is.' In case the newspaper's readers had not heard enough about the controversy, the last line of the article referred them to Mitchell's radio interview with family members at 8.30 am that morning.

Damian Honan and Angus Reed spoke to Mitchell during his breakfast show on 3AW. In a 25-minute interview, the sons-in-law spoke of the family's distress that Maritza had not acted to save Margaret and Paul's lives. Reed told Mitchell that: 'My children lost their grandmother and grandfather ... and perhaps had the right thing been done by common decency and someone had rung the police when they were bashed ... they might be alive today.'

Reed and Honan suggested that the family were willing to take 'further action' to answer some of their unanswered questions. Reed said, 'I can't come to terms with the fact that that isn't in any way a criminal act or in any way acceptable to the common man in the street [sic] ...' The men told Mitchell that the family had made a Freedom of Information Act application to get all the facts of the case.

Honan also said that he felt 'extremely upset and frustrated that as a parent and as a law-abiding member of society that we're not able to get an outcome from this that vindicates to us that society really cares in a way about the fact that these people were brutally murdered and may have lived had Maritza done the right thing'.

The Melbourne public relations firm, Inside PR, hired by the Wales family to handle their dealings with the media, was clearly doing its job by getting the family's concerns across. Before the plea hearing had started, everyone who was following the case knew that the Wales family was not satisfied with the fact that Matthew and Maritza had pleaded guilty to the charges laid and that they wanted further charges laid against Maritza and an inquiry into the events of 4 April.

It seemed that Matthew and Maritza's day of reckoning, as hampered by legal process and unsatisfactory as it may be, couldn't come soon enough.

CHAPTER 21

Pleading

18 December 2002

WHEN 18 DECEMBER DID ARRIVE IT WAS HOT AND HAZY WITH a brilliant blue sky. In Port Phillip Prison, Matthew rose early and lined up for a shower. He washed off the prison smell of dirty socks and stale men and dressed in a lime green shirt, a remnant from his more fashionable civilian days, and an expensively cut dark charcoal wool suit. Prison life had stripped the married life midriff from his body and he had regained some cheekbones. With his shaved head replaced by a new crop of thick dark brown hair, Matthew looked more like his mother's 'beautiful boy' than he had for years.

In her small unit in Kew, Maritza was up early too. She dressed herself with shaking hands. She had chosen a dark green suit with a plain blue knitted top underneath. The suit was sombre and unadorned, with loose pants and a long jacket. Her only jewellery was her plain gold wedding ring. She tied her long hair back in a ponytail and left her face bare. She looked serious and respectable. With her coffee Maritza swallowed two white pills, antidepressants prescribed by Dr Adler. Today, more than any other since this whole nightmare had started, she needed the numbness they gave her. She got Domenik ready and took him down the street to her parents' house. Over the last seven months, the little boy had been spending a lot of time with his surviving grandparents.

Matthew and Maritza arrived at the Supreme Court, a large domed sandstone building in the middle of Melbourne's legal district, at the same time. Matthew was brought up the cobbled back lane in a windowless, white prison van. Two protective services officers handed him over, with his hands handcuffed in front of his body, to four waiting uniformed police officers, two men and two women. They escorted him through the public corridors to Court Two.

At Court Two, the crowd had already started to gather. Matthew Wales walked through it with his chaperones. He was ushered through the wooden swing doors of the court, past his brother and sisters, who were waiting to go in. They studiously avoided looking at Matthew.

Once inside the court, Matthew was frisked for weapons and placed in the dock, a low oak pen which runs along the back of the courtroom facing the judge. Journalists and a court artist filled the press seats to the left of the dock.

Maritza arrived at Court Two through a side door. She was flanked by her legal team – Phil Dunn QC and his junior, Kate Rowe, Paul Galbally and Bernie Ahearn. Maritza walked past her in-laws and into the courtroom. She was frisked and led to sit next to her husband. She had not seen him since the last time they were in court and then they had been separated by a crowded courtroom. This was the closest they had been to each other since the day of their arrests.

The rest of the Wales family came into the courtroom. They milled around awkwardly for a few minutes and then sat in the three rows of bench seats behind the barristers. Tanned and well dressed in variations of black and white, the sisters had a thoroughbred look about them. Most families come to court wearing good clothes that wouldn't look out of place in a nightclub – a bit too shiny or see-through for the occasion. The Wales family got it right. Under the brown faces, the sisters looked tired and strained. They whispered quietly among themselves while the journalists watched them closely for any signs of reportable emotion. The Wales women kept themselves in check – sitting quietly and disappointing the reporters.

Court Two of the Supreme Court of Victoria is a courtroom untroubled by the twenty-first century. It has changed little since it was built in 1884. Located directly under the dome of the Supreme Court building, Court Two has oak panelled walls and hard wooden seats which offer little comfort to those who sit on them. Formally decorated in the Victorian tradition of pastel pink paint with white rosettes, Court Two has all the solemnity of a church and none of the spirituality.

In the upstairs public gallery, the narrow pews filled up by ten o'clock, half an hour before the plea hearing was due to start. Strangers, moved by a shared excitement, talked to each other. Their common interest in the case generated the kind of openness usually reserved for people who meet each other whilst travelling.

A former client of Matthew's told anyone who would listen that he used to cut her hair. She was very upset by the whole story. 'I can't believe he did it, he was such a lovely man. He was the best hairdresser I ever had. We used to talk all the time about everything. He changed when he met Maritza. He'd drop everything for her. She had him around her little finger. Then he just up and left the salon without any warning because she wanted him to start up a business. I missed him a lot. I read the papers and I couldn't believe it was Matthew; he wouldn't have done it if he hadn't met her.'

Next to the client sat another small grey woman in her mid-fifties. She was a friend of Margaret and Paul's housekeeper. She was keeping a proxy's eye on events because the housekeeper was too distressed to come herself. 'She doesn't think Matthew is a criminal yet,' said the friend.

A middle-aged couple who watch Supreme Court trials for amusement took a break from another case, a police shooting, to watch the plea. The woman said to her husband, and everyone else in her row, 'If this doesn't go the way it should, I don't know what I will do – I will be very angry. The judge has to do the right thing and lock them both up.' He nodded in agreement and wrote a note to himself, using capital letters, in his court-watching notebook.

Downstairs two police officers were guarding the door to the main part of the court. Only family members and the media were allowed in. Nervous expectation rippled among the spectators. By 10.30 am over one hundred people had settled in to watch the plea hearing. Others spilled out the door and down the worn stone steps. Most of the crowd were grey haired and well dressed – a biopsy of middle-class Melbourne. The buzz of excitement was so great, the audience could have been subscribers to the Melbourne Theatre Company and the plea the first play of a new season.

At 10.35 am, there was a loud knock from behind the wooden panels at the front of the court. Justice John Coldrey entered Court Two and sat on a large red leather chair at a high wooden bench. He looked out over the body of the court and up to the public gallery. Silence fell.

Coldrey had been a Supreme Court judge since 1991. Before

his appointment, he was the Director of Public Prosecutions for the State of Victoria. As Director, Coldrey was responsible for the prosecution of all serious crimes, including murder, in the state. A Queen's Counsel with a formidable reputation for his intelligence and wit, Coldrey was also known for his work for Aboriginal clients in Alice Springs and his interest in social justice issues. At sixty-one, Coldrey was grey headed under his white wig. He had a friendly face and sharp blue eyes. A fair judge with a touch of kindness, he was the sort of judge any defence barrister would be happy to draw for a plea hearing.

The judge's tipstaff, a retired army type dressed in a uniform of long green coat and white shirt, declared the court open. He had an officious air and a disproportionately strong sense of his own importance. The barristers sitting at the bar table in front of the judge announced their appearances, stating their names and those of their clients. On the prosecution side of the bar table sat Bill Morgan-Payler QC, Chief Crown Prosecutor for the State of Victoria, and his junior, Gabrielle Cannon. On the other end sat Michael Tovey QC and his junior counsel, Peter Morrissey, for Matthew; and Phillip Dunn QC and his junior, Kate Rowe, for Maritza. Opposite the barristers, facing the family, sat the solicitors – Kerry Maikousis from the Office of Public Prosecutions, Steve Pica for Matthew and Paul Galbally for Maritza.

The prosecutor started the proceedings by filing two presentments against Matthew and Maritza. The judge's associate read out the charges to each of the accused as they stood up in the dock: 'Matthew Robert Wales, the Director of Public Prosecutions presents that at Glen Iris on the 4th day of April 2002 you murdered Margaret Mary Wales-King. How do you plead?'

'Guilty,' replied Matthew.

'The Director of Public Prosecutions further presents that at

Glen Iris on the 4th day of April 2002 you murdered Paul Aloysius King. How do you plead?'

'Guilty.'

Damian Wales turned to look his brother in the eye – the rest of the family stared straight ahead.

The associate kept reading: 'Maritza Elizabeth Wales, the Director of Public Prosecutions further presents that at Armadale on the 9th day of April 2002, with intent to pervert the course of public justice you did an act which had a tendency to pervert the course of public justice in that you made a statement to members of the Victoria Police Force which falsely concealed your knowledge of the events surrounding the disappearance and murder of Margaret Mary Wales-King and Paul Aloysius King. How do you plead?'

Maritza replied in a voice just above a whisper. 'Guilty.'

The associate then told the judge that neither Matthew nor Maritza, now considered by the court to be 'the prisoners', had any prior convictions.

Justice Coldrey, resplendent in his red robes and whiter-than-white bib, leaned forward and addressed the Crown Prosecutor in a firm voice: 'Because there has been a great deal of public speculation and innuendo in this case, it is appropriate to know how the Crown case is put against each prisoner.'

Morgan-Payler, a tall and angular man in black silk robes and yellowed horsehair wig, moved to the lectern in the middle of the bar table. As a Crown Prosecutor with thirty years experience in criminal law, Morgan-Payler was ready for the request. He and Cannon had worked on the Wales-King case for months. Together they had read the 755 pages of witness statements, had conferences with the family and watched the three videos of the defendants' interviews with police.

'Your Honour, I intend to tender a number of exhibits and then do an opening.' Morgan-Payler handed up to the judge five thick books of police crime scene photographs and three video-tapes of the police interviews with the prisoners. The photographs became exhibit 'A'; the videotapes became exhibits 'B' and 'C'.

Morgan-Payler cleared his throat and began reading a summary of the crimes to the court. Three rows of family members, the twelve journalists, a court artist and the audience in the gallery, all sat in silence listening to the description of the victims' last dinner at the home of Matthew and Maritza Wales on 4 April. The prosecutor described the attack by Matthew on Margaret and Paul. He spoke about the family's frantic search for their mother and stepfather and the discovery of their Mercedes Benz in Middle Park on 10 April.

'On 29 April,' said Morgan-Payler, 'by sheer good fortune, the shallow grave was noticed by a park ranger in bushland off Woods Point and Warburton Road in Cambarville. The discovery was referred to the police and the bodies were exhumed.' Morgan-Payler told the court how the bodies were wrapped.

Morgan-Payler then described the autopsy findings. He read out Dr Dodd's conclusion that Margaret Wales-King had died of 'Blunt force trauma to head and evidence of asphyxia [sic]'. He said that she had suffered a laceration to her nasal bridge, a broken nose and extensive bruising to the right and back of her neck and upper back area. He then read Dr Dodd's opinion that 'those injuries are insufficient to cause death but are sufficiently forceful to lead to a state of reduced consciousness'.

Morgan-Payler then read from the pathologist's report, cold medical words that reduced the horror of the injuries: 'There were prominent haemorrhages on the right strap muscle at the base of the neck. This area of bruising is in direct continuity with

the bruising over the back of the neck and back of the arm sug-
gesting "manual neck compression". Strangling, Your Honour.'
Morgan-Payler paused for effect. The public gallery audience
shuffled on their uncomfortable seats. Morgan-Payler kept
reading: 'The brain was relatively well preserved and showed
some evidence of hypoxia or deprivation of oxygen. The victim
did not die immediately after the assault.'

Upstairs, people whispered. Even though they had read most
of the autopsy findings in the paper, the details sounded more
gruesome in the formal courtroom. Some explained what was said
in plainer terms than those used by the forensic pathologist. 'She
didn't die straight away.' 'He left her there alive.'

The family sat stony-faced looking straight ahead. Maritza
dabbed at her eyes with a white, folded, man's handkerchief. She
didn't look at her husband. His face was expressionless – the prosecutor could have been reading about someone else's deeds.

Morgan-Payler told the court that Dr Dodd had found paracetamol, codeine, and Atenolol (a medication for hypertension) in
Margaret's blood.

Morgan-Payler turned a few pages and read the results of the
autopsy on Paul King's body. The findings were quite similar.
Paul had patchy areas of bruising on his face, neck and arms and
a broken nose and broken bones in the middle third of his face
around the nose area. Once again, Dr Dodd found that the
injuries were not sufficient to cause death but almost certainly
rendered the victim unconscious. Morgan-Payler read Dr Dodd's
conclusion that it was entirely possible that Paul, like his wife, was
left face down unconscious in soft soil and had suffocated.

The Prosecutor told the judge that the toxicology reports on
Paul King's body revealed normal amounts of paracetamol and
codeine, but no Atenolol, in his blood and stomach contents.

Matthew had told police that he had put equal amounts of the crushed tablets into Margaret and Paul's bowls of soup.

Morgan-Payler then said that the police forensic team had found blood on the flagstones at the front of Matthew and Maritza's house and on the floor in their garage. He continued: 'The police had spoken to both prisoners on 9 April and both had given a false account of the evening's events. They both swore that Margaret and Paul had come for dinner, enjoyed it and then left.' Referring to the taped interviews between the investigating police and Matthew and Maritza, he told the court that both were interviewed on 11 May and had made full confessions. Matthew Wales admitted causing the deaths and that the killings were premeditated. He said that he decided a week or two prior to the murders to commit them and that his wife 'had no idea what was going on'. Matthew told police that the killing was triggered by the selling of the unit held by the family trust in Surfers Paradise.

Moving to the question of motive, Morgan-Payler told Justice Coldrey that clearly there were some disputes between mother and son to do with money. The prosecutor read out Matthew's description of his motive which had been replayed on the ABC news in October: '"Everyone would probably think that it was about money and it is about money, not for the use [sic] of me getting the money. It's the way she used her power for money, used money against Sally, Emma, Prudence, I'm not too sure about Damian, but she used it against me ... This anger that built up inside me, that they just wanted to alienate me from the family." When asked about Paul King, Matthew answered: "I liked Paul but he destroyed my mother and father's relationship too."'

As a prosecutor, Morgan-Payler had a duty to clarify for the judge what Matthew's intention had been when he attacked his parents. In case there was any doubt about this issue, Morgan-

Payler referred Justice Coldrey to the answer given by Matthew late in his interview: 'Yes, I intended to kill each of them when I struck them.' The prosecutor raised his head from his notes to look directly at the judge. 'The Crown says that these murders are in the more serious category because, for each victim, there was a specific intent to kill.'

Morgan-Payler read more from the interview. He said that Matthew told the interviewing police that he hit them on the back of the neck because he 'knew it would be quick'. He said that he struck them three times each and then, later in the interview, that he was 'going bananas – just kept hitting them'. He couldn't believe what he had done but was relieved it was over.

In response to a question about the marks found around his mother and stepfather's necks, Matthew told police that there had been no 'strangulisation [sic] at all' and that he only hit them on the back of the neck and they had died straight away. Morgan-Payler said as an aside that Matthew's answer was contrary to the opinion of Dr Dodd that both victims had survived the initial assault. There was a rustle of consternation amongst the Wales family.

Morgan-Payler summarised the steps Matthew took to move and bury his mother and stepfather's bodies and to disguise the grave site. Morgan-Payler finished his summary by telling the judge that the prosecution's view was that Matthew's account was not fully accurate. In barristerial code, Morgan-Payler was saying that Matthew had not been completely honest in his record of interview. He had answered the questions in a way that sought to protect himself from the full horror of his attack on his mother and stepfather.

Morgan-Payler said that it was important to note that the witnesses' statements, in the depositions, showed that when the search was going on for the missing couple, Matthew was not

greatly cooperative. It was only when Janet and Fred told police
that Margaret and Paul were going to Matthew and Maritza's for
dinner that Matthew Wales admitted to his worried family that
his parents had come to his house the night they disappeared.

> The Crown case is that Matthew Wales killed his mother
> and stepfather after contemplating it for a week or so, there
> was some degree of planning, he got the drugs, prepared
> and administered the substances to them in food and then
> killed them by, at least, striking them down and at the time
> he did so, he intended to kill them. Part of his motive was
> the relationship with his mother – the prisoner expresses
> some sense of injustice and bad treatment by the mother.
> This is no justification. There is no excuse, no underlying
> reason which mitigates the crime. In relation to Paul King,
> I submit, that the killing of him was necessary *simply
> because he was there*.

It is part of every prosecutor's role, when appearing in a plea
hearing, to remind the judge about the applicable sentencing principles. While prosecutors are not expected to suggest specific
numbers of years in prison or amounts of fines, they are expected
to outline the guidelines for sentencing which apply to the case. In
doing so, prosecutors like to refer to different 'scales' or categories
of criminal behaviour and place the offending act or acts within a
hierarchy of heinousness. Morgan-Payler discussed the sentencing
principles in relation to Matthew Wales's crimes: 'The Crown sub-
mits that the offences here reveal a higher category of criminality
and that there should be a substantial amount of cumulation of
sentence on the term of imprisonment.' In other words, Matthew
did not deserve a discount for killing two people at the same time.

Morgan-Payler put his pile of papers down and adjusted his wire-rimmed glasses. He took a sip of water from the glass in front of him. He had spoken for over an hour and not mentioned Maritza's role in the crimes. It was time to summarise her actions for the judge. Upstairs, some people took the opportunity to leave the gallery. Twice their number squashed into their places.

Now to the co-prisoner, Maritza Elizabeth Wales. She has pleaded guilty to one count of attempting to pervert the course of justice – that is making a false statement to police on Tuesday 9 April knowing full well that she had concealed her knowledge of events and the deaths of Margaret Wales-King and Paul King. She knew on Tuesday 9 April that her husband had killed two people and disposed of their bodies. On 11 May, Maritza made a statement to police in which she acknowledged that her earlier statement was false and saying that she had learnt the fate of the deceased on the night of 4 April. She then told police that she had seen the bodies in the front courtyard and did not know if they were alive or dead. She went upstairs and lay in bed while Matthew covered them up.

In her record of interview, Maritza told her interrogators that she did not know her husband was going to attack his parents and only found out that he had done so when she saw their bodies. She admitted that she had signed a sworn statement on 9 April and had informally told the police earlier that she did not know where her in-laws were. 'In these circumstances,' the prosecutor said, 'but for the remotest chance of the bodies being found, Maritza's statement may have meant that Matthew would escape liability. This is a *grave* example of an attempt to pervert the course of justice.'

Morgan-Payler finished off his part in the plea proceedings with some housekeeping matters – handing up draft orders to forfeit the items seized by police from Matthew's shed and asking the court's permission for the police to retain the DNA sample Matthew had provided earlier. He told the court that Matthew Robert Wales had spent 252 days in pre-sentence detention, including 18 December, and that ought to be taken into account when imposing a prison sentence upon him. He told Coldrey that Maritza, who was charged and given bail immediately, had not spent any time in jail.

The Chief Crown Prosecutor tendered his last exhibit. Exhibit 'D' was six Victim Impact Statements made by members of Matthew Wales's family. Victim Impact Statements are filed in a sentencing court by people affected by a crime. The judge is required to take the statements into account when determining the appropriate sentence. Because the victims of crimes don't play any other part in the plea hearing, the statements give them the chance, in their own words, to tell the judge how the crimes have impacted on their lives. To the disappointment of the audience, Justice Coldrey received the lengthy statements of Emma Connell, Prudence Reed, Sally Honan, Damian Wales, Elizabeth Wales and Di Yeldham, into evidence without asking the prosecutor to read them out. At 12.15, after one hour and forty minutes of talking, Bill Morgan-Payler closed the prosecution case, took his seat and sat back to watch his opponents.

Michael Tovey QC appeared for Matthew Wales with his junior, Peter Morrissey. Between them Matthew's legal team had clocked up more than thirty years in criminal law yet not one of them had ever seen a murder case like this. The media attention was unprecedented. It seemed that whilst murders were not that uncommon, a son killing his mother and stepfather was.

Tall and solid, Tovey has an imposing physical presence. In a voice quieter than expected, Tovey began his 'plea for mercy' for his client. A plea is the most creative part of a defence barrister's job. A plea done well is an art form, a piece of pure theatre that persuades and moves the audience. To make a plea effective, the barrister must weave the threads of their client's life together to make a tapestry of excuse, justification and sympathy. The aim of a plea is to reshape the most unsympathetic character into a likeable human being deserving of compassion.

Tovey's plea for Matthew Wales was a tale of a 'poor little rich boy' whose twin fates in life were to be intellectually deficient and obsessive. Tovey described Matthew, then 34, as a young man with a wife he adored and a young child he cared for. He also had a borderline IQ and few intimates. Tovey stressed that while Matthew was not intellectually disabled, he was clearly not the brightest star in the sky. He said that his client wanted to be regarded with respect, as anything other than the 'simple and dumb' baby of the family his siblings and mother saw.

Tovey didn't mince his words:

He killed his 69-year-old mother and 75-year-old stepfather. It appears, as time went by, Matthew came to obsessively focus on what he saw to be his mother's faults and what he saw to be things that she had done to him, which he thought had been hurtful. It would appear that this obsession, although it had probably been developing over a long time, really became more florid after his marriage in the late 1990s, to his wife Maritza ... he became very isolated within the marriage; he lost contact with his friends; he lost contact to a large extent with his siblings. He focused his attentions on his wife, whom he perceived to be just a wonderful person.

Behind Tovey, in the dock, Maritza wiped tears from her eyes. Tovey kept speaking:

It would seem that she [Maritza] wasn't wholeheartedly accepted by the family and there was a very large degree of tension arising from the fact that he had married her. And so it was that he came to focus on resentments, which may well have been previously not that significant in his life. But those resentments ... ultimately coalesced into a terrible obsession, whereby he came to look time and time again at what he saw to be his mother's faults. He felt that she was controlling his life, that she was unjustly manipulative towards him. That in fact, she didn't really love him but had always shown only a superficial affection and attention. He came to focus on the fact that he believed he'd been made the scapegoat for the breakdown of his mother's marriage, at the time that she took up with Paul King. He came to feel that his mother and indeed the whole family didn't value him as a person. He came to feel that he'd been alienated from and separated from his brother and sisters. He was extraordinarily anxious about the fact that he thought that his family and his mother looked down on his wife. That they thought that she was incompetent and not an appropriate wife.

Tovey explained to the judge that Matthew also thought that his mother was indifferent towards his son, Domenik, and that he was overwhelmed by a sense of subjugation and oppression by his mother. Matthew believed that the only way he could relieve the hurt he felt was to kill her.

Tovey pointed out that Matthew had thought about killing Margaret many times in the past. He had sharpened objects and

prepared nooses in ill-conceived plots to rid himself of her. Before
4 April 2002, the plots had never moved from thought to action.
The audience upstairs bristled with excitement. Despite the
extensive media reporting of the case, Tovey was telling them new
details, details that could be repeated with relish.

Tovey then described Matthew's relationship with his stepfather:

> Insofar as he took the life of Paul King, in his interview
> with the police he showed some sympathy for Paul King.
> The fact was that he, and indeed it would seem the whole
> family, really saw Paul King as no more than an extension
> of his mother. The overwhelming impression one receives
> from reading the statements and the interviews, is that
> Paul King didn't seem to have any presence independent of
> Margaret Wales.

Tovey argued that his client saw his mother's attitude to Paul
King as symptomatic of her attitude towards himself. He thought
his mother was capable of using both of them by faking her loving
concern for her own purposes.

Tovey then quietly dropped a bombshell. Those listening
strained to hear what he said. Tovey quoted the report prepared
by Ian Joblin, forensic psychologist, for the defence. He said that
Matthew had told Joblin that he had been touched 'inappropri-
ately' by Paul King when he was either nine or ten. A ripple of
shock ran through the public gallery. The journalists wrote
harder and faster in their little pads. The family moved uneasily
in their seats. Matthew simply looked down at his hands.

Tovey said that the inappropriate touching was not something
he was going to rely on as a motivating factor, but rather it was
'something in the background'.

'Certainly,' Tovey continued with some understatement, 'there was some degree of antipathy towards Paul King. Matthew was not close to him and resented him because he broke up his parents' marriage. Matthew felt that his mother treated his stepfather in a manner which was confirmation that she was self-centred and manipulative towards him.'

Conscious perhaps of the three rows of family sitting behind him, Tovey quickly assured Justice Coldrey that 'it is not part of this plea to denigrate Mrs Wales-King or to seek to cause the family any further pain. It is necessary however to refer to evidence which might explain how my client came to feel the resentments he did and to point to circumstances which existed, which might indicate that there was some factual basis for some of those resentments; even though, obviously, in the end their effect was blown out of proportion'.

Tovey wisely decided not to repeat the details of the killings. To do so would make his job of painting a picture of Matthew as a man who deserved some sympathy much harder. Rather, Tovey turned again to Matthew's motivation for killing his mother and stepfather. He used the answers in Matthew's record of interview with police to explain his client's actions. Using Matthew's own words gave the explanation greater resonance.

Tovey quoted Matthew's answers about his mother using her money as a tool to manipulate her children to do what she wanted. He listed some examples that Matthew gave the police of his mother manipulating him and his siblings. The two examples uppermost in Matthew's mind were the arguments with his mother over the profits from the sale of his house at 6 Horace Street, Malvern and the signing of the paperwork for the sale of his grandfather's unit in Surfers Paradise. Tovey told the court that Matthew had thought that his siblings would share his relief at his mother's death.

To flesh out the relationships between Margaret, Paul and Matthew, Tovey's junior barrister, Peter Morrissey, called the first of two character witnesses for Matthew. The first was a woman who, by virtue of a direction of Justice Coldrey, cannot be identified. She was the mother of a boy who was Matthew's friend when he was a seven-year-old Caulfield Grammar School student. She was chosen to give evidence on Matthew's behalf because she had spent a lot of time with him over a six-year period and could tell the court how isolated he had been. The woman was a credible witness who gave evidence, with a frank warmth and confidence, of things she had seen more than twenty-five years earlier. She and her son had seen Matthew every school day and some weekends throughout his junior school years. She had driven him to and from school and cared for him after school hours. Teachers at the school had approached her about Matthew's poor performance at school. The witness said that when she first met Matthew he had just moved to Caulfield Grammar Junior School, a co-ed campus, from Mandeville Hall, a co-ed junior school in a girls' school. For the first year the witness had driven Matthew to school he had asked her the same question: 'Am I a girl?' She had reassured him that he was not.

Morrissey asked her about Matthew's relationship with his mother.

'I didn't see them touch. It was a different type of relationship. I think Matthew did a lot of normal things with me, like going to McDonald's and just playing in the backyard, but I didn't see a closeness, quite frankly.'

The witness gave evidence that, whilst Paul King often picked Matthew up from her house, she thought the relationship between them was very distant. The witness was excused.

Morrissey called a friend of Matthew's from later years to the witness box. Michael John Ryan is a big bulky man, a nice guy who grew up in a less well-off environment and moved into the richer, faster Armadale set as soon as he could. Ryan was a seven-teen-year-old fresh from St Joseph's College, a scruffy catholic school in South Melbourne, when he became Matthew Wales's friend. Now 33, Ryan is a manager of a communications company and lives in St Kilda with two small children and a beautiful wife. He is one of only two friends who have made the trip to the visi-tors' room at Port Phillip Prison to see Matthew. Ryan told the court that, despite his crimes, he still considered Matthew to be a friend. Ryan and Matthew had shared a house in Armadale in 1994, many parties and holidays. Ryan gave evidence that on one of the holidays, at a Club Med resort in 1996, the two men found themselves at a bar talking about their families over a drink. Ryan was in full flight complaining about his father when Matthew interrupted him. 'At least you weren't molested.' Ryan told the court that his remark had stopped the conversation. The next morning Matthew begged Ryan not to repeat what he had said to anyone.

Morrissey asked Ryan some questions about Matthew's rela-tionship with Maritza.

'He was consumed by Maritza, and so much so that he prob-ably moved away from his group of friends . . . That he was – as I say, in awe. He – like I didn't see them – I didn't actually have that much to do with them together but when I did see them together he was very much the obedient husband.'

Ryan was excused and Tovey continued his plea, turning to the relationship between Maritza and the Wales family. He said that Matthew felt, with good reason, that his family did not accept his wife and that they did not respect her business skills. Tovey read Emma's statement to police in which she described Maritza as a 'vulgar little guttersnipe'. The journalists, knowing good copy when they hear it, made sure they wrote that phrase down. The next day it was repeated in all the papers.

The QC gave Justice Coldrey an extensive summary of Matthew's school and work history. He tendered a recent report by psychologist Raymond Smith who had seen Matthew in 1984 for counselling about his lack of direction, motivation and maturity. Smith remembered that Margaret had been protective of Matthew and defended him publicly when he was marginalised by his siblings. Smith concluded his report with a prophetic comment: 'My impression is that all of the Wales children except Matthew were achieving satisfactorily. Further, that Matthew's history was that if it were possible for things to go wrong, they would. From memory, Margaret felt exploited by Matthew, but nonetheless protective of him.'

Dr Lester Walton, forensic psychiatrist, had visited Matthew briefly in his first few days in jail. He had prepared two reports for the defence, dated 29 August and 9 December. Tovey tendered them to the judge. Walton had referred to Matthew's intense hatred of his mother and his minimal regret over killing her.

Tovey then called Ian Joblin to the witness box. The forensic psychologist was well known to Justice Coldrey and was relaxed giving evidence. Joblin told the court that he had seen Matthew nine times at Port Phillip Prison, had administered a number of psychological tests and had prepared two reports, dated 20 September and 9 December, based on the information he had gathered. The reports were tendered. Joblin gave evidence about Matthew's IQ of 83 and his skewed view of reality when it came to his relationship with his mother. Joblin told Coldrey that Matthew had developed an obsessional drive to rid himself of Margaret, as he perceived her to be the cause of extreme psycho-

logical abuse. He said that after the killings, Matthew had felt
overwhelming relief. Joblin said that he did not think Matthew
had any remorse for the murders but rather was psychologically
satisfied after he had committed them. He did not consider
Matthew to be psychopathic or a danger to others. Joblin told the
court that Matthew was placed in the Marlborough unit at the
prison with the other prisoners who could not function in the
mainstream unit of the jail. Joblin said that prison staff were concerned that Matthew would become depressed and possibly
suicidal in the future.

Morgan-Payler got up to cross-examine Joblin. He asked him
some questions to get the forensic psychologist to confirm that
Matthew did not have any remorse for his actions. Joblin readily
agreed with that. He also agreed with the prosecutor that
Matthew's intense feelings and limited intelligence made a very
troubling mixture. At 4.40 pm, Joblin was excused from the witness box and Justice Coldrey closed the court for the day.

19 December 2002

At 10.35 am, Court Two reconvened. The family took up the
same seats as they had the day before and once again the public
gallery was packed. The morning papers had carried the first
day's proceedings on their front pages and Melburnians were
eagerly waiting the next instalment.

Tovey did not let the media attention bother him. He had
come to the end of his plea and had to address the judge on the
issue of an appropriate sentence. Matthew, he submitted, could
not be sentenced on the basis that he was motivated by greed.
Tovey told Justice Coldrey that while the killings were deliberate,
Matthew had no plan beyond them and had taken steps to make

sure the victims suffered as little pain as possible. He said that his client considered that his confession to the crimes was inevitable. 'He was conscious that he'd committed a terrible crime, he was conscious that it was proper that he should own up to what he'd done and he was conscious that he deserved significant punishment for what he'd done.'

Tovey said that the judge did not have to consider the sentencing principle of deterring others from doing the same thing to be of great significance when sentencing Matthew because it was such a rare crime for a son to kill his mother. Tovey did not talk about the killing of Paul. Matthew's good work record, his lack of any prior convictions, his lack of a history of violence and the fact that he was not a danger to anyone else all meant, Tovey submitted, that his crimes were not the worst example of their kind but rather fell in the middle range. At 10.50 Tovey sat down; his job was done.

*

When Phillip Dunn QC stood up in Court Two at eleven o'clock on the morning of 19 December he wanted to achieve two things for his client, Maritza Elizabeth Wales. He wanted to 'keep her home' and he wanted to make the media revise their thoughts about her.

Dunn began by handing up to the judge a folder containing a chronology of his client's life, two medical reports and some employment records. He then went straight to his main point: 'How does one categorise this offence and how one categorises the offence in relation to Matthew Wales, has an impact on Maritza [sic] . . . Why on earth would Matthew Wales kill his mother?'

Dunn's main concern, in arguing that Maritza Wales was deserving of compassion, was to distance her husband's actions, killing his parents, from her own – covering up for him. He needed therefore to persuade Justice Coldrey that the heinous nature of Matthew's crime should not exaggerate the gravity of Maritza's crime of providing one false statement to the police. Any judicial abhorrence towards Matthew should not rub off on Maritza.

Dunn reminded Coldrey that Matthew's killing of his parents was a crime born out of a mixture of low intellect and obsession; that he did not have financial gain as his motive and that Maritza was an unwilling participant in the ensuing events: 'He doesn't think like a normal adult. He doesn't. And what that means is this: that when he did what he did, which was a thoughtless, stupid, horrible thing to do, he catapulted all around him into a nightmare. He catapulted his wife and son into a nightmare. He catapulted his own family into a nightmare.'

Dunn told the court how Maritza was shocked when she found out what Matthew did and she fell back on her 'old-fashioned values' of 'family and respect and respect for law and order as well'. Her first instincts were, he said, to tell Matthew to go to the police. Matthew had asked her to give him time and she did. Ultimately however, Dunn said, Maritza saw her lawyer, Paul Galbally, and provided her 'can say' statement to the Homicide Squad *before* the arrest of Matthew Wales. 'She feels guilty about that.' Dunn continued. He had the full attention of every person in the courtroom:

> Your Honour, the fact is, and as you've seen from those medical reports, that it took some time for the realities of the situation to settle in for her and no doubt she was asking Matthew, as she said and he said, to go to the police – but what she did on 9 April, and this is what she's charged with, is that she has made one false statement. She made it

in circumstances where her husband was asking her to, where she was no doubt shocked and traumatised by what had happened and when the police officers came to her, she didn't go to the police, the police came to her ... and she told them, amongst other things that what had happened is that Mr and Mrs Wales-King had left. She didn't add to it and she didn't amplify it, and though she was spoken to by police, I'm told as they came to the shop and particularly to the house, on all occasions her husband was present.

Dunn then went through the answers Matthew gave in his record of interview about what he told Maritza after he killed his parents and how she responded. His account accorded with the answers Maritza gave to police in her interview. Both said that Maritza had asked Matthew to go to the police straight away, that she continued to beg her husband to do the right thing and that she knew nothing of Matthew's plan to kill Margaret and Paul.

Dunn then moved on to an area that had become controversial since Matthew's siblings had been quoted in the media asking for Maritza to be charged for her part in the murders, or at least for her inaction once she discovered the bodies in her front garden.

And the question [quoting from the record of interview]: 'Why didn't you get help for Margaret and Paul?' I didn't want to know. I didn't want to touch anything. I didn't want to know what happened, nothing. I didn't want to know why he didn't want to. I was scared. I know Matthew has done wrong but I was scared.

Question 674: 'Why didn't you tell the police what happened?' Because I was thinking of Domenik. I was thinking of everything except for the right thing. I don't know, but I tried, I tried so many times. I said to Matthew, please – I keep on saying to him, like, we're putting Domenik through hell. I said, I can't handle it. Deep in myself I couldn't, but you know, I went to tell – when I went to tell my – I tried to go on Wednesday and I went to the city and so on.

Dunn read out another part of the interview which explained his client's feelings further.

But the question is: 'What did you hope you'd achieve by providing a false statement?' Answer: 'Scared, scared of losing Matt, scared of losing Domenik, just, I feel like I'm being pulled from left, right and centre. I didn't know what to do.' We do know, Your Honour, despite her divided loyalties, she did go to the police prior to her husband's arrest.

Dunn moved on to an area that had bothered him about this case – the inordinate amount of negative media attention his client had received. At the mention of the media, the journalists scribbling in the front row of the press seats in the courtroom looked up.

What overshadows this case – dark shadow, really, that hangs over this case – and this case has got enough that is horrible about it already – has been the unfortunate media publicity, a large amount of which appears to have been engendered by the Wales-King family and their hired public relations firm. I don't know what the purpose of going on the radio, or the purpose of hiring a public relations consultant, is for this family, but they have, amongst other things, made public comments saying they'd be unhappy if Maritza got a suspended sentence ... This family has deployed their money and their hired public relations guns to revile this woman publicly when she is incapable of defending herself. I don't know what pressure they propose to bring on this court or Your Honour –

At the mention of any possibility of the court being pressured, Justice Coldrey interrupted Dunn mid-sentence: 'I don't know how far we need to pursue this ... I have not read much of the material in the press but I can assure you and persons present that I'm not subject to media pressure and I'll sentence in this case both of the offenders based on the facts as I find them, based on their personal histories, and in accordance with the principles enunciated in the Sentencing Act.'

The lecture was as much a message to the Wales family as it was for Dunn's benefit that the Judge was independent and would not be influenced by outside pressure.

Dunn set out the details of Maritza's background emphasising that she was a migrant woman who had moved from her family home to her husband's house at the age of thirty-five; that she was adored by Matthew and, until the murders, had lived a quiet life of hard work and domesticity which had 'old-fashioned values' as its fulcrum. The media reports before the plea hearing had mentioned that Maritza had undergone surgery for breast augmentation. Dunne knew that breast implants and 'old-fashioned values' were an uneasy mix. He told the court that Matthew had arranged for Maritza to have breast implants after she had finished breastfeeding their son.

The picture Dunn painted of Maritza, the wife and mother, was a vastly different one from that reported in the media prior to the plea hearing. Until Dunn stood up that morning the only view of Maritza conveyed by the press and television news was one of a greedy, conniving wife who had loaded a metaphorical gun and handed it to her dim-witted husband to pull the trigger. Much was made of her 'sex kitten' demeanour and her breast implants and her inaction once she saw the bodies of her in-laws in the garden. Angus Reed and Damian Honan, Margaret's sons-in-law, had asked, in the radio interview on 5 December with Neil Mitchell, why she hadn't been charged with murder. The Wales family clearly felt that their sister-in-law was the root of all evil in their family and had urged Matthew to kill his mother and step-father.

Dunn turned to the crux of his plea – the request for Maritza to receive a sentence that enabled her to remain at home with her son:

> Her son will turn three next March. He's lost one parent and a parent who had a lot to do with him. He needs his mother. That little boy needs his mother. She is perhaps the only person right now, other than his elderly grandparents, that he's centred around. He doesn't understand why his dad doesn't come home. He's been asking why his dad doesn't come home. He's been asking, will Father Christmas bring Dad home? And Father Christmas is not going to bring his father home ...

Dunn argued that Maritza making a false statement was not excusable but was understandable given her background and her position as a wife and mother. He also listed her plea of guilty, her previous good character and her eventual cooperation with the police as factors in favour of giving her a suspended jail sentence.

At 12.05 pm, he concluded his plea with a flourish: 'It's wrong to do what she did, but having done it she's paid a pretty heavy price as you can see from those medical reports [they detail a history of depression, anxiety and feelings of guilt] and somehow or other she's got to get on to the next bit of her life and hopefully that is looking after that little boy. If the court pleases.'

Dunn's plea for mercy for Maritza was nearly eight months in the making yet it took only a little over an hour to deliver. His style was theatrical and passionate. Most of the audience were moved and persuaded despite their best intentions not to be.

After the plea was over, Dunn received telephone calls from journalists congratulating him for changing their way of thinking about Maritza. He had, they admitted, persuaded them to see her as something other than an evil, scheming woman setting her husband up to kill his parents.

As for keeping Maritza at home with Domenik, it would take a little longer to find out if that aim had been met, for Justice Coldrey would not sentence Maritza until after the January legal vacation. The traditional month-long summer holiday, however inconvenient for the other participants in the criminal justice system, was sacrosanct. It was to be four months before anyone listening in Court Two found out whether Dunn got what he asked for.

CHAPTER 22

Sentencing

11 April 2003

ONE YEAR AND ONE WEEK TO THE DAY AFTER MATTHEW murdered his mother and stepfather, he and Maritza returned to the Supreme Court of Victoria to receive their sentences. After a week of brilliantly sunny autumn days, Friday 11 April was marked by grey skies and torrential downpours. The city streets were awash with water and black umbrellas. The sombre mood in Court One matched the weather.

Neither the passage of time nor Australia's involvement in a war in Iraq had diminished the public's interest in the case. Since the plea hearing, the Wales-King murders competed with national bushfires and the war to be reported three times. In February, the *Herald Sun* ran two stories. The first was that Matthew's 'socialite' former fiancée had been found. A large photograph of Fleur Lauber accompanied the article.

A week later the same newspaper ran a story about the sale of 40 Mercer Road for a reputed $1.5 million. The property had been for sale since July 2002 and was privately sold in the middle of February. In an effort to deter the simply curious, the real estate agent who organised the sale, Margaret's son-in-law James

Connell, had prospective buyers make appointments to inspect the property.

Finally, a small article reported the sale of the Surfers Paradise unit which had caused Matthew such anguish. As the convicted killer of his mother, Matthew was barred by law from getting any of the sale proceeds.

On the morning of the sentencing, both Melbourne's newspapers published articles reminding readers of the facts of the case and that the day of sentencing had arrived. The newspapers need not have worried. Melbourne had not forgotten Matthew and Maritza. The public gallery was filled long before the sentencing was due to start at 11 am. Some of the audience had been there for the plea hearing and wanted to watch the final instalment for themselves. Others had made the effort to visit the court because the media reports had made them curious. A security guard turned people away at the door. Not even the weather had dampened Melbourne's interest in the most exquisitely juicy family drama it had ever had the pleasure of watching.

The Wales family came into court before Matthew and Maritza. For them the last part of the criminal justice puzzle would never signal the end of the tragedy. Since the plea hearing, they had endured their first Christmas without their mother and stepfather. Their ten young children had all had a birthday without their grandparents and had also lost contact with an uncle, an aunt and a cousin. No matter how much they had tried to have a normal summer at Portsea and Sorrento, Margaret's four oldest children still had days filled with grief and anger.

The family sat, as they had during the plea, in the front rows behind the barristers. Each of Matthew's siblings and their spouses had returned for the sentence. All were formally dressed and grim-faced. Emma, James Connell, Prue and Angus Reed took the front seats and Damian and Elizabeth Wales, Sally and Damian Honan sat behind them. Their summer tans had faded a bit and the strain of the last few months was written on their faces. Sally was bent forward in her seat clutching onto her husband's arm. Prue had a set of rosary beads in her hand. Throughout the sentence she rubbed the little silver balls as if they would give her the strength to bear what she was hearing. Di Yeldham sat behind her youngest nieces. Before the sentencing started, she turned her immaculately groomed head to glare at her nephew in the dock.

Matthew did not react to his aunt's scorn. For the first time in months he was sitting next to Maritza. The couple, both dressed in dark suits, were placed together in the wooden dock. The smallness of the dock meant that there was no room for a protective services officer, or security guard, to sit between them. Matthew could finally touch his wife.

Matthew had spent the past four months keeping his head down in the Marlborough Unit at Port Phillip Prison. He worked for six dollars a day. The only good thing about his time there was that each day spent waiting for Coldrey's sentence was counted as a day towards fulfilling his term of imprisonment. By Friday 11 April, Matthew had spent 336 days in prison. He had not had a visit from Maritza on any one of them.

Domenik was never going to have his dad home for Christmas. Phil Dunn's efforts at the plea hearing meant that he had at least spent the summer with his mother and her parents. Like his cousins, he had celebrated his first birthday without his paternal grandparents, turning three just two weeks before his parents' sentencing. Domenik didn't see his father for his birthday.

Since the plea hearing, Maritza had been living in Kew waiting for the last step in the criminal justice process to be completed.

The only remaining mystery about the case for her was whether or not Justice Coldrey was going to lock her up. Maritza, along with the rest of Melbourne, was under no illusions about what her husband's family thought she deserved. The Wales family had made it clear in the media that they thought she had played a larger role in the murders than that revealed by the charge she was pleading guilty to and they wanted her to be jailed.

As for Matthew, Justice Coldrey's decision wouldn't change his accommodation – the only question was how long he would stay there.

At 11 am, the wait was over. There was a loud knock on the oak panels and Justice Coldrey came into court and took his place on the bench. For the next hour and twenty minutes, he read his judgment from a prepared document.

The judge started by summarising the crimes committed by Matthew and Maritza. When handing down a sentence, a judge has an obligation to set out the facts upon which he or she relies to determine the appropriate penalty. In most cases the judge recites a short summary of the facts. In passing sentence Justice Coldrey was careful to set out, in much greater detail than usual, the facts upon which he relied. The twelve journalists in the press seats to the left of the court wrote down his every word. Coldrey took his summary from the depositional material and the psychological reports filed in the court.

He spoke for an hour, referring extensively to the witness statements and the records of Matthew and Maritza's interviews with police. Coldrey remarked upon the consistency of the couple's accounts of the night of 4 April 2002. Coldrey stressed that he was relying on the facts as uncovered by the investigating police. The judge looked up from the typed document before him at the family sitting in the body of the court. He repeated that the version of events found in the depositional material provided the basis for the sentence he was about to give. In other words, the judge was warning that the media reporting or the family's version of events would not influence his determination of the appropriate penalty for the two accused. Justice Coldrey spoke for nearly an hour, attempting to put to rest all the gossip, rumour and speculation that had besieged the case since its first days.

Coldrey repeated the facts of the killings, the autopsy results and some of the subsequent Homicide Squad investigation. He noted the steps that Matthew took to dispose of the bodies and cover up the killings. He said that Matthew's lies and deceptions during the investigation greatly increased the anguish of the rest of his family. Coldrey said that Matthew had developed a deep hatred for his mother, perceiving that she had used her money to dominate and manipulate his life. He said that he accepted that the killings were not motivated by greed or a desire for money. The judge referred to Ian Joblin's report in which the forensic psychologist concluded that Matthew had a 'skewed reality' which developed into an obsession about his mother's treatment of him. Coldrey quoted Joblin's conclusions that the killing of Margaret and Paul became Matthew's ultimate expression of financial and emotional independence and that afterwards he felt relief. Coldrey described the killings as premeditated. Despite this, he said that Matthew's lack of planning about how to dispose of the bodies, the Mercedes and the bloodstains in his front yard gave the murders 'all the hallmarks of a poorly thought out solo enterprise'. Coldrey said that he found that Maritza Wales had played no role in the killings and that her husband's actions had placed her in a horrific position.

The judge made a point of commenting that it must not be forgotten that Margaret Wales-King had the right to use her money as she wished. He also said that Matthew's complaints of ill treatment must be considered in the context of a privileged upbringing which included access to farms, beach houses, a unit in the snow and numerous trips overseas.

After reading his summary, Coldrey stressed that what he had described were the facts as known compared with the public misperceptions that had surrounded the case. He repeated that there was no evidence linking Maritza to the murders of Margaret and Paul and the killings were solely the result of Matthew's obsession. There was a loud gasp from someone in the family rows.

The judge said that the depositions revealed the family's dislike of both Matthew and Maritza and that he thought that the statements of the Wales siblings contained a great deal of hearsay and retrospective opinions. The court, the judge said, was only concerned with Matthew's perceptions of his mother.

Justice Coldrey then turned to the relationship between Matthew and Paul King. He said that Matthew had told police that he liked his stepfather and that three of his siblings said that they thought he was close to Paul. The judge said that the accounts Matthew had given of the sexual abuse he suffered from Paul had 'significant discrepancies' in them and that Matthew's barrister for the plea hearing, Michael Tovey QC, had not relied on the allegations. The judge said that he rejected Matthew's claim of sexual abuse and found that Matthew had killed his stepfather because he was frustrated with him for being dominated by his mother and because he was a witness to the killing of Margaret.

Coldrey then summarised the psychological material filed during the plea hearing. He said that both Dr Walton and Ian Joblin found that Matthew was free of any psychological disorder. He noted that Walton's report mentioned that Matthew had fantasised about building an electrocution device to kill his mother. Joblin's report spoke of Matthew sharpening sticks and making nooses for her murder.

While the summary was being read out, Maritza lowered her head and sobbed in great open-mouthed, silent gasps. Matthew rubbed her knee for comfort and whispered in her ear. Maritza avoided his eyes and kept looking everywhere except at her husband's face. In the family seats, the sisters shook their heads and sighed. Emma wrote a note to Prue. Prue read it and nodded and then went back to rubbing her beads.

Coldrey took a sip of water and moved on to the legal rules known as sentencing principles. By law, a judge is bound to apply these when determining a sentence. Before handing down a sentence, it is customary for a sentencing judge to describe how the principles apply to the case before him or her. Coldrey was obliged to consider the issues of specific and general deterrence, Matthew and Maritza's prospects of rehabilitation, whether they had any remorse for their crimes, the fact that they had pleaded guilty and their previous character.

Moving through the mitigating and aggravating aspects of the crimes, Coldrey addressed his remarks to Matthew and Maritza. He said to Matthew that the aggravating features of the case were that the victims were elderly and very vulnerable, that the murders were premeditated, that he went to extensive means to cover up the murders, that his conduct after the killings caused great anguish for his family and that he had no remorse for the murders. On the mitigating side, Justice Coldrey found that Matthew had a low IQ and could not control his obsession, he was no real threat to the community generally and therefore the principle of specific deterrence, that is of deterring Matthew from killing again, did not really feature in the sentencing equation. The judge

also said that it was significant that Matthew had no prior convictions, no history of violence, was a good father and had a good
employment record. He was, in the judge's mind, a person with
good prospects of rehabilitation. The judge also gave Matthew
and Maritza a 'discount' in their penalties for their pleas of guilty.

Justice Coldrey looked at Maritza and said that he was satisfied that she had no role in killing Margaret Wales-King and Paul
King and that her husband had placed her in an unexpected,
extraordinary situation. She had faced a conflict between what her
husband wanted her to do and what was legally correct. The
judge said that it was clear from a report filed on behalf of
Maritza written by her psychiatrist, Dr Adler, that she was suffering a severe grief reaction to the events of the last year and that
she was taking antidepressant medication to cope with her
ongoing guilt about going to the police and her anxiety and distress caused by the massive amount of media scrutiny. On the
credit side, the judge said that it was pertinent that Maritza had
come forward to the police and that she had previously lived a
blameless life as a hardworking, ordinary person. Her rehabilitation prospects were excellent. Coldrey said that, in reaching a
sentence for Maritza, he took into account that she had pleaded
guilty, that her psychiatrist was concerned for her health in prison
and that she was the carer of a young boy. He also considered that
she had remorse for her actions, had already suffered publicity
and that her marriage had been destroyed by her contact with the
police.

Finally, after talking for over an hour, the judge moved to the
part everyone in Court One had come to hear – the penalty. The
judge sentenced Maritza first.

He said, taking into account the circumstances of her offence,
he sentenced her to a two-year term of imprisonment to be

suspended for a total of two years. 'Such a sentence,' Coldrey said looking at Maritza over the top of his half-glasses, 'would give you the opportunity to look after your child.' The sentence meant that Maritza would stay out of jail provided she committed no further serious crimes during the next two years. If she did reoffend, the two-year jail term would be activated and she would be incarcerated.

At this there was shaking of heads, in disbelief, and murmurs of consternation amongst the Wales family. Maritza kept sobbing. For the first time throughout the sentencing, she moved her hand to rest lightly on her husband's.

Coldrey looked at Matthew. 'I sentence you, on count one for the murder of Margaret Wales-King, to twenty years imprisonment and, on count two for the murder of Paul King, to twenty years imprisonment. Ten years of the sentence on count two will be cumulative on the sentence for count one, making a total effective sentence of thirty years. I declare that you must serve twenty-four years before being eligible for parole . . . Remove the prisoner. Adjourn the court.'

As one, Matthew's siblings turned to stare at him in the dock. The hatred on their faces could be felt upstairs in the public gallery. The audience shrank back behind the wooden balcony, ashamed at being caught in a moment too private to be witnessed by strangers. Matthew was led out of the court to a waiting prison van parked in the wet, cobbled lane that ran down the side of the old court building. Two photographers rushed to capture one last image of Matthew as he stepped into the white van. When Matthew Wales next steps out into the real world, he will be 58 years old. Maritza will be 62 and his toddler son, Domenik, will be 26.

The media scurried to the main Supreme Court entrance on William Street to try and interview the family. A crescent of umbrellas shielded the camera crews and reporters gathered at the bottom of the sandstone steps. David Wilson, the representative hired by the Wales family, came down the steps and addressed the media. For a public relations man, he spoke quietly. He asked those gathered not to pressure the family as they left the court. He alluded to the judge's remarks that some of the family were on medication and were still suffering the psychological effects of the crimes. After Wilson went back inside the court, one cameraman turned to a reporter and said, 'Fuck them, I'm not moving.' The media pack stayed put.

A few minutes later, the Wales family walked down the stairs. Damian Wales, pale and tired and dressed in a light green jacket and cream shirt, stepped forward and addressed the assembled media. He said that the family thanked the court for its help and that there were still some questions that needed to be answered about the killings. Damian said there were some anomalies in the materials uncovered during the police investigation. 'This whole case has been dictated by what my brother and sister-in-law have had to say. There is more to it.' Damian told the media that a formal statement would be provided later. The family walked across William Street and into a building of barristers' chambers. A few of the cameramen and reporters followed them. Once they had crossed the road, a 'friend of the family' who had sat in on the sentence told those who were left that the Wales family were determined to spend their every last cent 'getting Maritza'.

Detective Inspector Andrew Allen of the Homicide Squad stepped in front of the microphones after Damian and the rest of his family had crossed the road. The detective said that, as far as the Victoria Police were concerned, the case was over, the investigation was concluded and the matter solved thanks to the hard work of the investigators. When pressed by reporters to comment on the family's feelings, Allen replied that if they had concerns, they could take them to the Director of Public Prosecutions. 'But for now,' he said, the police would 'get on with those murder cases that hadn't been solved'.

Before the media dispersed, David Wilson handed out a typed statement on behalf of the Wales family. The document set out the family's feelings of frustration and anguish that the 'full facts and truth' behind the murders had not been uncovered. The statement highlights the conflicts and inconsistencies contained in the depositional material and calls for a coronial inquest, 'open and public in nature', as the family's 'only chance of achieving closure on this tragedy'. The family stated that they wanted a chance to challenge and question the 'lies and untruths' so 'obscenely directed at our mother and stepfather'. They believed that a coronial inquest would afford them that opportunity even though it may cause more pain and suffering. At the end of the statement, the family requested that their privacy be respected in the hope that they could move forward with 'peace and dignity'.

That night, for the first time in a month, the ABC seven o'clock news displaced the reporting on the war in Iraq to run a story on the sentencing. The next morning, the readers of the *Herald Sun* would be woken with the front page headline 'As killer son is jailed for 30 years and wife walks free, angry family says "She won't get a cent"' followed by five pages of text, tables, a chronology and photographs connected to the Wales-King murders.

The rain drenched the camera crews as they followed Maritza leaving the Supreme Court's side door onto Lonsdale Street. Paul Galbally and the junior barrister, Kate Rowe, walked beside her. Maritza walked the few hundred metres to her solicitor's office in William Street surrounded by a gaggle of photographers, cameramen and reporters. She covered the entire distance in silence, looking straight ahead. All around her, drivers stuck in the wet weather traffic honked their horns and passengers leant out to see who was attracting the flash of the cameras. Pedestrians turned as Maritza and her entourage walked past. In amongst the media scrum and the lunchtime traffic, Maritza walked straight-backed and calm, into the rain and the rest of her life.

Epilogue

IN JUNE 2002, ONE MONTH AFTER THE BODIES OF MARGARET and Paul were discovered, a couple in Malvern held a dinner party for some friends. It was a highly organised affair with a mini Louis Vuitton handbag marking the ladies' and a mobile phone marking the men's place settings. The menu was printed and placed at each setting. The dinner party had a theme – the Wales-King murders. The food was described by reference to the details of the killings. The host served 'French onion soup or thirty finely ground Panadeine Forte' followed by 'Fillet of Beef and shallots or bang 'er and smash 'im'. For desert there were 'Little lemon pots and coconut macaroons or sticky little pillows (these are guaranteed to take your breath away)'. A quiz on the facts of the case was printed on the inside of the menu. The diners and hosts considered the dinner a great success and still remember it with laughter.

A few months later, before Matthew and Maritza were sentenced, other residents of the Armadale, Malvern, Glen Iris circle were walking around in the dark with torches and a guide. They were on a Wales-King walking tour. It took in Matthew's house at

1/152 Burke Road, Glen Iris. Now occupied by the owner, it had not visibly changed since it was a crime scene in April and May 2002. The walkers may or may not have been told that the house's owners tried to sell it after their tenants' arrests, without success. They hired a spiritual cleanser to rid the property of evil spirits. He performed a cleansing ceremony but left unsatisfied because, although he found the house to be clean, the front courtyard remained resistant to his efforts.

The tour also visited the Mobil service station where Matthew hired the trailer, to the High Street shop where Maritza ran Maritza's Imports and finished at 40 Mercer Road for a look at Margaret and Paul's final home.

Each year in Australia there are 340 murders. Twelve of these victims are parents killed by their children. Of them, five are mothers.

One month after the Supreme Court sentenced Matthew Wales for killing his mother and stepfather, it sentenced Giuseppe Russo, a 39-year-old unemployed fitter and turner, for killing his Italian-born migrant mother and father in the ugly, factory-fringed, western suburb of Altona. Russo used his crippled father's walking sticks to bash him to death and smashed his mother's face to pieces against the concrete of her back step. The victims left an estate worth $200 000. Throughout their lives they had bought their son two properties and a car. Russo killed his parents because he felt that they should have given him more financial assistance.

Russo did not feature on the front pages of the Melbourne newspapers. His crimes and his sentence of 28 years jail received only a few paragraphs of comment. Nobody much remembers his case. There are no Russo dinner parties or walking tours around Altona.

The Wales-King murder case received more media attention than any other killings in Melbourne's history. It did so because the Wales family is rich and because the killing of one's mother is still taboo.

From the first words printed about the disappearance of Margaret Wales-King and her husband Paul King, the public knew they were wealthy. They knew that their silver Mercedes Benz was also missing and that it was worth $130 000. They knew that the couple had travelled from their expensive home in the affluent suburb of Armadale to have dinner (rather than 'tea') with their family in Glen Iris and had never come home. They knew that the couple were handsome and that they had nice looking, middle class children who were worried sick about them and were able to articulate that worry in a police media conference. It was obvious, by the way the family presented to the media and the photographs of Margaret and Paul in their evening clothes, that their disappearance was unlikely to be related to the criminal underworld or to the taking of drugs or too much alcohol. Placing the disappearance outside the usual reasons for people vanishing meant that the story was instantly a real mystery, Christie-esque in its characters and satisfyingly disturbing for any armchair detective.

Dr Muriel Porter, coordinator of RMIT University's Graduate Diploma in Journalism, blames the family's wealth for the public and media obsession with the story. Porter sees the case as a modern fairytale in which a jealous son kills the beautiful queen and her king so that he can be free. She says that if Maria and her second husband Paolo from the working class suburb of Footscray went missing and their beaten-up Torana was found abandoned at Highpoint City Shopping Centre in Melbourne's western suburbs, neither the media nor its consumers would have been interested. The case of Russo proves Dr Porter's point. However, the media alone cannot be blamed for the level of interest in the case. According to Dr Porter, it was simply reacting to the public's obsession with it. She believes that the case unconsciously tapped into themes that have fascinated the populace since ancient times. She notes that all Greek tragedies were about important people with status, money or position within society who experienced hardships.

The Wales family is of an influential class. Margaret and Di were well known in upper middle class society in Melbourne and Sydney. The Wales siblings went to large private schools that are close to their childhood and adult homes. The family's social circle was both large and narrow; it revolved around a small number of suburbs within Melbourne's inner eastern suburbs. Geographically small but demographically powerful, the circle encompasses Toorak, Camberwell, Hawthorn, Armadale, Malvern and Glen Iris. It is bordered by Melbourne's oldest and most expensive private schools. The schools generate a subculture of Melburnians who, for the most part, all know each other, are generally financially well off and live lives shaped by the routines of the wealthy – the races, the ski season, summers at the coast and running children around to private schools. The theory that everyone in the world is connected to each other by six degrees of separation is reduced in the Wales family's area of Melbourne to two degrees. Nearly everyone in the upper middle class in Melbourne was one or two steps removed from the story. For those in their class, the case was simultaneously repulsive and attractive. The Wales were both people like them and unlike them, familiar in their ways yet enmeshed in a tragedy that was shockingly alien. The tension between their similarities and dif-ferences created the obsession with their story. For those within and those outside their class, the case was followed with a degree of schadenfreude. They shared a malicious glee that all the money, glamour and other-worldliness of the Wales family did not mean that it was perfect.

Catharine Lumby, Director of the Media and Communications Programme at Sydney University, agrees with Porter in ascribing the public's fascination with the case to the fact that the family is rich. She says that their lives represent our own aspirational fantasy of what a family can be, or can have, and for that reason we are intensely interested in what went wrong. In Lumby's view, the public are shocked by the fact that a person like Matthew Wales committed such horrible violent crimes: his actions upset the cosy presumption that people who do that sort of thing come from an aberrant world, not the leafy streets of Armadale, Camberwell and Glen Iris. Matthew's killings show that even in an 'ideal' family, it is possible for very unattractive characteristics – evil, hate, anger, murderous obsession and frustration – to ferment and erupt with devastating consequences. Lumby believes that Matthew's deeds were riveting because they stripped away the public's denial of the level of anxiety, drama and trauma that exists in the nuclear family.

Dr Priscilla Pyett, a sociologist at the University of Melbourne, believes that issues of class are also at the root of the public's fascination with the case. In her view, the way the disappearance and investigation were reported meant that the public could read about another class when following the case. The notion of 'class travelling' was a theme in another well-reported murder case in Melbourne, that of toddler Jaidyn Leskie. When he disappeared from his mother's boyfriend's house in the economically depressed town of Moe in Victoria's La Trobe Valley (cruelly nicknamed 'Latrine Valley'), media consumers could, perhaps for the first time, enter into the miserable lives of the working class protagonists from the comfort of their own homes.

In the Wales-King case, the journey was to a more luxurious but equally interesting class. The media fascination with the details of the case, the family's lifestyle, their views of Maritza and their concerns about the outcome of the legal proceedings, meant that more information than usual was published. Much of the family's private business became public knowledge. In an era where reality television swamps our lounge rooms, the Wales-King case was reality soap, drama of the highest order. By watching the drama, the audience was given insights into the upper class, a demographic not known for its exposure of secrets.

The way the story unfolded ensured that interest in the case would increase rather than wane as time went on. In true mystery style, those watching were never disappointed. From the first days of the disappearance, the audience was hooked and the ensuing drama played out as beautifully as any well-written script. The plot's points, finding the car, discovering the bodies, arresting a family member, were tantalisingly laid out – just close together enough to sustain interest but not too close to diminish the mystery.

The readers of Melbourne's daily newspapers weren't just reading through the details of the investigation, they were looking for clues. In their reporting, the newspapers played the role of investigator as well as publisher. For days before Matthew and Maritza were arrested, the media had singled them out for attention. Headlines such as 'Son weeps at mother's funeral' meant that Matthew's position as the main suspect for the killings was one of Melbourne's worst kept secrets. The stories published became a form of media 'Cluedo', a mystery game for all to play. Sadly, the case wasn't a game for the rest of the Wales family.

Chris Maxwell, the President of Liberty Victoria, a civil rights organisation, thinks the media went too far. In an article published in *The Age* in the week after Matthew and Maritza's arrests, he asked: 'By what right does a newspaper assume the role of investigator and prosecutor?' The public interest, he argued, is not served by the publication of details of the police investigations but rather by the preservation of the integrity of the criminal investigation process and the right of any person under suspicion to be presumed innocent until proven guilty and to have privacy. Maxwell was also concerned about the effect of the saturation of media coverage on the grieving Wales family. 'The right to grieve in private is not a commodity to be traded in the media marketplace. It is not a residual right to be enjoyed only after media consumers have had their fill. It should be the first thing, not the last, on the editor's list of priorities.'

In amongst the media frenzy about the case, there was no broader analysis of what makes men kill their mothers. It happens so rarely in this country that there are no Australian studies of the phenomenon. However, a small number of clinical studies in Britain provide a summary of common features in matricides. They are usually committed by young men who either live at home or close to their mother, are unmarried or have difficulties in heterosexual relationships and who have an intensely dependent relationship with their mother. The murdered mothers are usually perceived by their killers to be overly dominating, possessive, interfering and controlling. More often than not, men who kill their mothers have lost their father through death or divorce and therefore the intensity of the child-and-parent bond is increased. The relationship between mother and son is usually fraught with subservient hostility and they often argue over 'food or money'. The killer commonly benefits from the mother's interference while simultaneously complaining that his mother's treatment of him is humiliating. In the majority of matricides studied, the killer was psychologically ill at the time of the attack with either schizophrenia or depression and was sentenced to hospital detention rather than jail. Unlike Matthew, most men who kill their mothers do not have siblings or at least do not have very many of them.

Matthew Wales's record of interview with the police reveals a man who shares many of the characteristics of others who have committed matricide. He rants and raves against his mother's dominance in his life and sobs about her controlling nature. Matthew's father, Brian Wales, left the family home when Matthew was seven. His relationship with his son after the divorce was virtually nonexistent. There were reports of Matthew asking Brian Wales if he was his father or his uncle. Matthew said that Paul King was not a substitute father and that he was no more than an extension of his mother.

Psychoanalysts have spilt much ink on the matricidal theme in myths and literature. One of them, Wertham, in a 1941 study of men who killed their mothers, coined the phrase 'Orestes complex' for the set of psychological factors that precede matricide. Wertham took the name from the Greek myth of 'Orestes' by Euripides, in which Orestes, a young man, killed his mother under the influence of his sister. In the story, the motive for the killing was the death of Orestes' father.

Wertham's Orestes complex arises when a son has an ambivalent relationship with his mother (which later turns into rage); there is a crisis in the relationship in which the son has a sense of overwhelming emotion and that translates into an immediate need to act and kill. For Wertham there is one more factor superimposed on the rage – a sexual desire for the mother. Later psychoanalytical interpretations of the myth cite the murder of a mother as a final attempt by the murderer to break away from a dominating mother figure and become independent.

Certainly Matthew Wales fits within some of the criteria for Orestes complex. He had an intensely ambivalent relationship with his mother and felt only relief when he had killed her. Like other mother-killers, he saw himself as breaking free from the constraints of his relationship with his mother and ready to emerge into adulthood and 'normal life'. For Matthew the act that brought him psychological freedom robbed him, and the rest of his family, of ever having a normal life again.

Appendix

Friday 11 April 2003

STATEMENT ON BEHALF OF THE WALES KING FAMILY

We are greatly disturbed that the investigation and sentencing process has not uncovered the full facts and truth behind the horrific murders of our mother and step-father.

The process completed today had the purpose of sentencing our brother and sister-in-law who pleaded guilty to certain crimes.

The process was not to uncover the full facts of the cause and method of death.

There are conflicts and inconsistencies in the documents included in the police brief, the forensic evidence and the transcripts of the pre-sentence hearing.

The Crown Prosecutor noted that the version of the events provided by our brother to police and in the pre-sentence hearing was not necessarily "an accurate version of events" and that there were a "number of puzzling features" in the case.

Tragically, the confession of our brother today stands as the so-called factual account of the details and reasons behind these brutal crimes. To us, his account was self-serving and based on selfish opportunity and selfish greed.

We believe we have a right to the full facts. We believe the public has a right to know. We cannot accept that selfish opportunity and selfish greed should replace proper process and proper investigation to determine and finalise the full outcome of this tragedy.

None of us can properly deal with the pain of this tragedy until we have the facts.

We believe that a coronial inquest must be held as soon as possible. An open and public inquest is our only hope of achieving closure on this tragedy. We need that closure. Our children need that closure. So will their children. And, surely the public must have absolute confidence that such heinous crimes do not solely and abruptly end on the confession of a proven liar, but are then at least tempered and balanced by the facts and truth that can be pursued by thorough and rigorous investigation, examination and proper judicial process as provided for by an open and public coronial inquest.

Such an inquest might bring more pain and suffering. While our extended family has suffered enormously over the past 12 months, we have remained silent to the litany of lies and spurious allegations that have been made against our loving, cherished and devoted mother and step-father in the great hope that the full facts will be eventually known.

Indeed, we have had no legal right or recourse to even question, let alone challenge, the lies and untruths so obscenely directed at our mother and step-father. A coronial inquest would provide that opportunity.

Our family cannot rest until every appropriate step is taken towards uncovering all the facts.

Finally, while we understand and appreciate the media and public interest in this matter, we ask for our privacy to be respected in the hope that we and our 10 children can move forward with peace and dignity.

For confirmation:

David Wilson
Director, Inside Public Relations

Michael Smith
Director, Inside Public Relations

This document was handed out on the steps of Owen Dixon Chambers after the sentencing on Friday 11 April.

Endnotes

The events recreated in this book are taken from statements provided to police by the individuals involved and, in some cases, in interviews with the author. Any discrepancies between accounts are a result of the natural differences in perception of those telling the story.

Chapters 1 and 2

The events recorded in Chapters 1 and 2 are recreated from the Records of Interview of Matthew Wales and Maritza Wales with Homicide Squad detectives on 11 May 2002 and from discussions between the author and Ian Joblin, forensic psychologist.

Chapter 3

Direct quotes are attributed within the text and are from statements given to police by Damian Wales on 2 June 2002, Emma Connell on 4 June 2002, Brian Wales on 2 June 2002, Sally Honan on 13 April 2002 and 29 May 2002, Prudence Reed on 20 June 2002, James Connell on 14 April 2002, Angus Reed on 16 April 2002.

The author has not named any of the Wales family grandchildren.

Chapter 4

Direct quotations are attributed within the text and are taken from statements made to police by Sally Honan on 13 April 2002, Damian Wales on 2 June 2002, Emma Connell on 10 April and 4 June 2002, Prudence Reed on 12 April 2002 and 20 June 2002.

General information has been obtained from the author's interview with Ian Joblin, forensic psychologist.

Chapter 5

Direct quotations are attributed in the text and are taken from statements to police by Emma Connell on 4 June 2002, Damian Wales on 2 June 2002, Sally Honan on 29 May and 30 May 2002 and Prudence Reed on 20 June 2002.

General information is taken from Matthew Wales's and Maritza Wales's Record of Interview with police on 11 May 2002.

Chapter 6

Direct quotations are attributed within the text and are taken from statements to police by Emma Connell on 5 June 2002.

General information and direct quotes have been obtained from statements to police made by Emma Connell on 9 April 2002, 4 June and 5 June 2002 and 11 June 2002; by Damian Wales on 2 June 2002; by Diana Yeldham on 4 July 2002; by Janet Roche on 16 April 2002; by Frederick Roche on 16 April 2002; by John Van Hewerdin on 9 April 2002; by Sandra Ingpen on 19 April 2002; by Sally Honan on 13 April 2002 and 29 May and 30 May 2002; by Prudence Reed on 20 June 2002; by Damian Honan on 12 April 2002; by Rebecca Jones on 28 May 2002; by Sharon McCrory on 28 May 2002; by Craig Shiell on 24 May 2002; by Stephen Sheahan on 28 May 2002 and by Andrew Hodgson on 25 May 2002.

Chapter 7

General information has been obtained from Matthew and Maritza Wales's Records of Interview with police on 11 May 2002 and from statements to police by Sally Honan on 29 May and 30 May 2002; by Amanda Kidson on 6 May 2002 and 3 July 2002; by Scott Turley on 3 May 2002; by Julie Hayes on 17 May 2002; by Teresa McGlashan on 3 May 2002; by Andrew Morrison on 13 May 2002; by Geoffrey Powell on 4 May 2002; by Glenn Bigger on 17 May 2002; by Jamie Tonkin on 6 May and 9 May 2002; by Craig Lamont on 9 May 2002; by Alexander Rance on 17 May 2002 and by Carol Geier on 16 May 2002.

Chapter 8

General information has been obtained from statements to police by Jamie Tonkin on 6 May and 9 May 2002, by Craig Lamont on 9 May 2002 and from Matthew Wales's Record of Interview with police on 11 May 2002.

Chapter 9

General information has been obtained from Matthew and Maritza Wales's Records of Interview with police on 11 May 2002.

Chapter 10

General information and direct quotes have been obtained from statements to police by Sharon McCrory on 28 May 2002; by Craig Shiell on 24 May 2002; by Narelle Fraser on 17 July 2002; by Stephen Waddell on 11 July 2002; by Henry Van Veenendaal on 19 July 2002; by Peter Cox on 5 June 2002; by Stephen Lake on 10 June 2002; by Maritza Wales on 9 April 2002; by Matthew Wales on 9 April 2002; by Prudence Reed on 12 April and 20 June 2002; by Damian Wales on 9 April 2002 and by Emma Connell on 9 April 2002.

'are people you wouldn't . . . It is a baffling mystery.' '. . . we have driven the streets . . . We are very fearful for them.' *The Age* 'Who would harm charming couple?' 4 May 2002

Chapter 11

General information has been obtained from statements to police by Tracey Starr on 27 June 2002; by Narelle Fraser on 17 July 2002; by Mark Hester on 10 April 2002; by Jim Blyth on 12 April 2002; by Christopher Pountney on 19 May 2002; by Brad Newton on 17 May 2002; by Stuart Bailey on 14 May 2002; by Craig Shiell on 24 May 2002; by Stephen Waddell on 11 July 2002; by Sally Honan on 29 May and 30 May 2002; by Charles Mouratidis on 19 April 2002 and by Emma Connell on 4 June and 5 June 2002.

'Missing couple's Mercedes found' by Tanya Giles and Russell Gould, *Herald Sun*, 11 April 2002, page 3.

Chapter 12

'They were buying dips . . . had to be helped', *Herald Sun,* 12 April 2002.

'Please, just give us some sort of clue . . . we want their bodies', *Herald Sun,* 16 April 2002.

General information and quotations attributed in the text are obtained from statements to police by Henry Van Veenendaal on 19 July 2002; by Stephen Waddell on 11 July 2002; by Sally Honan on 29 May 2002; by Brian Wales on 2 June 2002; by Prudence Reed on 20 June 2002; by Angus Reed on 16 April and 18 April 2002; by Emma Connell on 5 June 2002; by Di Yeldham on 4 July 2002; by Craig Shiell on 24 May 2002; by Robert Nazaretian on 12 June 2002; by Narelle Fraser on 17 July 2002; by Amanda Kidson on 6 May 2002; by Stephen Lake on 10 June 2002; by Deborah Ryan on 22 July 2002; by Howard Hopper on 18 July 2002 and from Matthew Wales's Record of Interview with police on 11 May 2002.

Chapter 13

General information has been obtained from statements to police by Jon Gwilt on 29 April 2002; by Alan Caddy on 29 April 2002; by Wayne Phillips on 19 May 2002; by Peter Cox on 5 June 2002 and by Charlie Bezzina on 11 May 2002.

Chapter 14

General information and direct quotes have been obtained from statements to police by Malcolm Dodd (two Autopsy Reports) on 12 July 2002; by Stephen Waddell on 11 July 2002; by Narelle Fraser on 17 July 2002; by Henry Van Veenendaal on 19 July 2002; by Melanie Archer on 19 June 2002 and by Pamela Craig on 17 July 2002.

Chapter 15

General information and direct quotes have been obtained from statements to police by Emma Connell on 11 June 2002; by Narelle Fraser on 17 July 2002; by Prudence Reed on 20 June 2002; by Sally Honan on 29 May and 30 May 2002; by Stephen Waddell on 11 July 2002; by Robert Nazaretian on 12 June 2002; by Stuart Cameron on 20 June 2002; by Andrew Stamper on 12 July 2002; by Peter Knox on 28 June 2002, by Howard Hopper on 18 July 2002 and from Maritza Wales's Record of Interview with police on 11 May 2002.

Chapter 16

Direct quotations are attributed in the text and with general information have been obtained from police statements by Damian Wales on 2 June 2002; by Di Yeldham on 4 July 2002; by Emma Connell on 11 June 2002; by Gerard Curtain on 18 June 2002; by Kevin Rees on 4 July 2002; by Scott Turley on 3 May 2002; by Brian Wales on 2 June 2002; by Jamie Tonkin on 6 May and 9 May 2002; by Teresa McGlashan on 3 May 2002; by Geoffrey Powell on 4 May 2002; by Sally Honan on 29 May and 30 May 2002; by Andrew Stamper on 12 July 2002; by Stuart Cameron on 20 June 2002; by Julie Hayes on 17 May 2002; by Glenn Bigger on 17 May 2002; by Narelle Fraser on 17 July 2002 and by Henry Van Veenendaal on 19 July 2002.

'courteous but trembling', *Herald Sun*, 4 May 2002

'the first stage is out of the way … we've actually got a result', *Herald Sun,* 4 May 2002.

'The tributes were not immune . . . further on in the same paper', *Herald Sun*, 4 May and 7 May 2002, *The Australian*, 8 May 2002 and *The Age*, 3 May, 4 May, 7 May and 8 May 2002.

'That morning . . . soon after the disappearance', *Herald Sun*, 8 May 2002.

'they believe may have been used to . . . after they were murdered', *The Age*, 8 May 2002.

'"Goodbye – Son's tears for murdered mother" . . . before the service', *Herald Sun*, 9 May 2002.

'That morning . . . were the last to arrive', *The Australian*, Friday 10 May 2002.

'Until recently . . . St Kevin's College', *Parish History*, St Peter's Toorak, provided by the church to the author.

'His voice broke . . . had died', *Herald Sun*, 10 May 2002 and *The Australian*, 10 May 2002.

'smart lot, the men in suits . . . still in their gym gear', *The Sunday Age*, 12 May 2002.

'After the visit, Damian . . . and mourning session', *The Weekend Australian*, 11 May 2002.

'Outside the church . . . and comforted each other', *The Australian*, 9 May 2002 and *The Age*, 9 May 2002.

'Family mourns as suspicions swirl', *The Australian*, 9 May 2002.

'A final word in a chapter of their lives . . . where they deserved to be', *The Sunday Age*, 12 May 2002.

Chapter 17

Direct quotations are attributed in the text and with general information were obtained from the author's interview with Phillip Dunn and conversation with Robert Richter.

Michael Tovey QC was eventually briefed to appear, without conditions, for Matthew Wales.

Chapter 18

Direct quotations and general information obtained from Matthew and Maritza Wales's Records of Interview with police on 11 May 2002 and from statements to police by Stephen Waddell on 11 July 2002; by Narelle Fraser on 17 July 2002; by Henry Van Veenendaal on 19 July 2002; by Robert Nazaretian on 12 June 2002; by Anthony Joyce on 29 May 2002; by Di Yeldham on 4 July 2002; by Prudence Reed on 12 April 2002 and by Sally Honan on 13 April 2002.

Chapter 19

Direct quotations and general information obtained from author's interviews with Ian Joblin.

Chapter 20

Direct quotations are attributed in the text and are taken from Neil Mitchell's interview on 3AW radio station on 5 December 2002 and from the statements to police of Brian Wales on 2 June 2002; by Stephen King on 20 June 2002.

General information has been obtained from the Melbourne Magistrates' Court records

'achieved a level of notoriety . . . justice in this state', *The Age,* 14 May 2002.

'Nevertheless . . . an avalanche of media reports.' For example: *The Australian.*

'Tears as eyes meet at murder hearing', *The Age,* 14 May 2002.

'Son in court over parents' murder', *The Illawarra Mercury,* 14 May 2002.

'Wales faces exclusion from will, if convicted', *The Age,* 15 May 2002.

'Did you kill our mother? The question Wales family put to their brother', *The Sydney Morning Herald,* 18 May 2002.

'You fucking rot in hell, whore.' *The Age*, 18 October 2002.

'I think it's grabbing ... to the point isn't it?', *The Sunday Age,* 20 October 2002.

'done a lot of harm ... There is a lot more to it', *Who Weekly,* 4 November 2002.

Chapter 21

Direct quotations are attributed in the text and have been obtained from the Transcript of Plea Hearing for 18 December and 19 December 2002.

General information has been obtained from the author's interviews with legal personnel.

Chapter 22

Direct quotations are attributed in the text and with general information are taken from the Transcript of Sentence of Justice John Coldrey and from the Media Statement released by the Wales family on 11 April 2003. A copy of the Statement is contained in the Appendix.

Epilogue

General information about the dinner party and walking tour has been obtained by correspondence between the hosts and the author in May 2003.

General information about homicides in Australia has been obtained from the National Homicide Monitoring Programme, Australian Institute of Criminology's 'A Study of Family Homicides in Australia 1989/90 to 2001/02' by Catherine Rushforth and Jenny Mouzos.

For further information on the Russo killings see R v Russo [2003] VSC, Sentence dated 22 May 2003.

General information from Dr Porter, Dr Lumby and Dr Pyett was obtained from their interviews with the author in December 2002 and February and March 2003.

For further information on the studies of matricides in the United Kingdom and the work of Wertham, see Christopher Green, 'Matricide by Sons', *Medicine Science Law* (1981) Vol 21, No. 3, page 207; F Singhal and A Dutta, 'Who Commits Matricide?', *Medicine Science Law* (1992) Vol. 32, No. 3 page 214; and S Clark 'Matricide: the Schizophrenic Crime?', *Medicine Science Law* (1993) Vol. 33, No. 4, page 326.

'"Son weeps at mother's funeral" ... Melbourne's worst kept secrets', *Herald Sun,* 8 May 2002.

'by what right ... investigator and prosecutor?', *The Age*, 14 May 2002.

Acknowledgements

My heartfelt thanks to Sue Hines and Andrea McNamara at
Allen & Unwin for opening the door and to Ray for lovingly pushing
me through it; to Heather and Alan, to Helen and Wal for the room
of one's own; to Suzie; to Anna; to Rebecca; to Katie; to Louise;
to Susan; to Helen M; to Craig; to Helen G; to Kath; to Gillian;
to Stephen, Jane, Sally, Louisa, Stuart, Rosie and Caroline for their
myriad acts of support and kindness and to those involved in the
case who graciously gave their time and information in order
to make the story as accurate as possible.

Photographic Credits

COVER

Front cover: On 8 May 2002, youngest son Matthew Wales sheds a tear at the funeral of his mother Margaret Wales King and Paul King who were found murdered in bushland near Melbourne (photographer Trevor Pinder, Newspix).

Back cover: Convicted murderer Matthew Wales at the Supreme Court in Melbourne, 11 April 2003, for sentencing over the deaths of his mother and stepfather (photographer David Crosling, Newspix); Maritza Wales, on a charge of attempting to pervert the course of justice, leaves Melbourne Magistrates Court, 2 September 2002, after a hearing (photographer Fiona Hamilton, Newspix).

ILLUSTRATED SECTION

Damian Wales, Prudence Reed and Emma Connell plead for help to find their mother and stepfather, 10 April 2004 (courtesy of Newspix).

Cover of the booklet for the Memorial Service of husband and wife, Paul King and Margaret Wales-King in Melbourne, 9 May 2002 (courtesy of Newspix).

40 Mercer Road, Armadale (courtesy of the author).

Margaret Wales-King's Mercedes parked in Middle Park (courtesy of the Freedom of Information Unit, Victoria Police).

1/152 Burke Road, Glen Iris (courtesy of the author).

Inside the fence of 1/152 Burke Road, Glen Iris (courtesy of the Freedom of Information Unit, Victoria Police).

Matthew and Maritza Wales and their son return from shopping to their Glen Iris home, 6 May 2002 (courtesy of Newspix).

Maritza Wales outside her store in Armadale, 3 May 2002 (photographer Kristi Miller, Newspix).

Matthew Wales's Nissan Patrol and hired trailer (courtesy of the Freedom of Information Unit, Victoria Police).

Markers showing blood stained pavers outside Matthew Wales's front door (courtesy of the Freedom of Information Unit, Victoria Police).

Aerial view of the bush grave where Margaret Wales-King and Paul King were buried (courtesy of the Freedom of Information Unit, Victoria Police).

Senior-Sergeant Charlie Bezzina inspects the bush grave of Margaret Wales-King and Paul King in the Yarra Ranges National Park, Marysville, 30 April 2002 (courtesy of Newspix).

The child's wading pool and bricks found in the bush grave (courtesy of the Freedom of Information Unit, Victoria Police).

Friends and family at the funeral of Margaret Wales-King and Paul King, 8 May 2002 (photographer Craig Sillitoe, Fairfax).

Matthew Wales arrives at the Custody and Remand Centre for an out of sessions hearing, 11 May 2002 (photographer Cameron L'Estrange, Newspix).

Sister of Margaret Wales King, Di Yeldham, leaves the Magistrates Court, 2 September 2002 (photographer Fiona Hamilton, Newspix).

Accused killer Matthew Wales arrives at Victorian Supreme Court, 18 December 2002, charged with the double murders of mother Margaret Wales-King and stepfather Paul King (photographer Fiona Hamilton, Newspix).

Maritza Wales leaving court, 11 April 2003, after the sentencing of her husband for the murder of his mother and stepfather (photographer Sharon Walker, Newspix).